KU-675-927

YOU CAN WALK TO FITNESS
RACHEL ARMSTRONG

NEW
HOLLAND

Dedication
To Kevan, Ben and Robyn

First published in 2007 by
New Holland Publishers (UK) Ltd
London • Cape Town • Sydney • Auckland

www.newhollandpublishers.com

Garfield House
86–88 Edgware Road
London
W2 2EA

80 McKenzie Street
Cape Town 8001
South Africa

Unit 1, 66 Gibbes Street
Chatswood, NSW 2067
Australia

218 Lake Road
Northcote
Auckland
New Zealand

Leabharlann Chontae Laoise

Acc. No. GS8/SA7S

Class No. 613.71

Inv. No. 9929

WITHDRAWN

Copyright © 2007 in text: Rachel Armstrong
Copyright © 2007 in illustrations: New Holland Publishers (UK) Ltd
Copyright © 2007 New Holland Publishers (UK) Ltd

Rachel Armstrong has asserted her moral right to be identified
as the author of this work.

10 9 8 7 6 5 4 3 2 1

All rights reserved. No part of this publication may be reproduced, stored
in a retrieval system or transmitted, in any form or by any means,
electronic, mechanical, photocopying, recording or otherwise, without
the prior written permission of the publishers and copyright holders.

ISBN 978 1 84537 998 8

Editorial Direction: Rosemary Wilkinson
Commissioning Editor: Ross Hilton
Copy Editor: Clare Hubbard
Designer: Paul Wright
Illustrator: Stephen Dew
Production: Marion Storz

Reproduction by Modern Age Repro House Ltd, Hong Kong
Printed and bound by Replika Press Pvt Ltd, India

The author and publishers have made every effort to ensure that all
information contained in this book was contained at the time of press.
They accept no responsibility for any loss, injury or inconvenience
sustained by any person using this book or the advice given within it.

Contents

Introduction

I am a competitive athlete and am constantly trying to find ways that I can improve my times – whether it's by paying more attention to my diet or my technique, getting more sleep or training smarter. I am fortunate to have a fantastic coach to help me get the best out of myself, a supportive husband who doesn't mind me disappearing off to events all over the world and two lovely children to whom I hope I offer some kind of inspiration to get out there and have a go!

I am also a personal fitness trainer which puts me in the very privileged position of being able to help other people achieve their goals and aspirations. I hope that through this book I can help you on the way to achieving yours.

Our lifestyles seem to be getting more and more hectic. We are, I believe, becoming 'technologically overloaded' and it's not without consequence. We have gizmos for this, gadgets for that, computer programs to make life 'easier' – everything is digital, and mobiles and emailing have made it almost a crime to be unavailable. It's not good for us! Some of my most enjoyable training sessions with clients are the ones that start with the words 'I nearly called you to cancel today', because I can guarantee that these will be the sessions that end with the words 'I'm so glad I came!' That's not down to me, it's the beauty of exercise.

Quite often these sessions start with a walk. Everyone can walk and it always amazes me how quickly people relax after just a few minutes. Walking, especially in natural surroundings, gives us a real feelgood factor, as well as being great aerobic exercise. It needn't cost a penny bar a decent pair of walking shoes either. What I have set out to do in this book is to give you some ideas and inspiration so you can start walking yourself to fitness.

You can have more energy, you can lose weight, you will feel more confident and you will tone and strengthen your body by following a walking programme. All you have to do is decide that you want to.

So, what are you waiting for?

CHAPTER 1
WHY WALK?

Human beings have been walking for around 4 million years. For our ancestors walking was a necessity to fetch water and food, to build shelter or simply to move to a different area – all of which could involve walking many miles. Fortunately these days we don't need to go to quite these lengths in order to survive! We can drive to the supermarket in a matter of minutes with no real physical effort involved. Our bodies are designed to exercise – activity is good for us, whilst inactivity is positively bad for us. There really is nothing like putting on your walking shoes and going out for a good walk, not just to get fitter but also to cleanse and invigorate the mind. So, there's a very simple answer to the question 'why walk?' Because it's good for you.

Walking is good for your:
- Heart

- Lungs

- Blood

- Metabolism

- Muscles and joints

- Mind

- Wallet!

Who can do it?

Anyone and everyone who can put one foot in front of the other – from tiny toddlers to great grandma. The beauty of walking is its simplicity. There is no complicated technique to learn and you don't need lots of expensive or specialized equipment.

Physical benefits

A healthy heart

Walking briskly gives your whole cardiovascular system – that's your heart and lungs – an excellent workout. The moment you step out of your front door and start walking, even at a fairly modest pace, your body's requirement for oxygen increases rapidly. To meet this demand the heart, which is a muscle, must pump harder and faster in order to supply oxygen-rich blood to the working muscles. If this happens on a regular basis, for example as part of a new walking programme, your heart will start to adapt like any other muscle, so that the challenge becomes easier. Over time it gets a little bigger and stronger so that more blood can be pumped out in each heartbeat. In addition to this, blood vessels to the heart itself get bigger so there is an improved blood supply to it. All of these changes mean that not only is the risk of having a heart attack reduced, but the chances of surviving one are better too. You will also find that your resting heart rate (see box below) drops a little, which is another indication that your heart has become more efficient.

What is resting heart rate?

Resting heart rate is how many times your heart beats each minute when you are at rest. The best time to check it is in the morning soon after waking, before you have anything to eat or drink and the stresses of the day kick in, as any of these things will increase your heart rate. The easiest way to check it if you don't have a heart rate monitor (see page 34) is by placing the pads of your index and middle fingers on the side of your neck just under the jaw bone. Once you can feel a pulse, count the number of beats in 15 seconds and then multiply by 4. This is your resting heart rate.

Look after your lungs

Put simply, your lungs are responsible for getting oxygen from the air that you breathe into your blood and taking waste carbon dioxide out. At rest, we don't use our lungs to their full capacity because we don't need to. The problem is that if the lungs aren't challenged they begin to lose their elasticity and the muscles which are involved in breathing weaken. This can mean that even relatively light exercise causes breathlessness in some people. Aerobic exercise like walking causes the lungs to take in up to ten times more air than at rest, and subsequently the lungs and breathing muscles become more efficient.

Did you know?
Your lungs weigh in at around 1 kilogram and if you were to spread them out the surface area would cover an entire badminton court!

Healthy blood

Regular exercise helps to keep blood 'clean' and the arteries and veins healthy too. Inactivity, along with other factors such as poor eating habits, stress and genetic factors, can mean that levels of cholesterol build up in the blood.

What is cholesterol?

Cholesterol is found in all cells of the body and we need a certain amount for good health, but excess cholesterol ends up in the bloodstream and is carried around via high-density ('good', 'HDL') or low-density ('not so good', 'LDL') lipoproteins. LDLs carry cholesterol from the liver into the tissues so that it can be used in cell maintenance, but if there are too many LDLs, cholesterol is 'dumped' in the bloodstream causing fatty deposits in the blood vessels, a bit like limescale builds up in a kettle. Eventually this can cause a blood vessel to narrow so much that it becomes blocked. If this happens to a vessel supplying the heart or brain, the result may be a heart attack or stroke. HDLs, on the other hand, actually 'steal' cholesterol from the blood and take it back to the liver. Regular exercise reduces the levels of LDLs and increases the levels of HDLs, lessening the chances of these fatty deposits settling in the blood vessels. Clear blood vessels also mean lower blood pressure; high blood pressure is another major risk factor associated with heart attacks.

Keep the blood circulating

Walking involves rhythmic contraction and relaxation of muscles which improves circulation by helping to squeeze blood back to the heart. This is especially true of muscles like the calves which act as a pump with each step. This contraction and relaxation of the muscles also helps to boost the lymphatic system which is important for the immune system.

Circulation of blood to the skin is also improved during exercise as a way of cooling us down. This delivers oxygen and nutrients to the skin better than any facial treatment and helps to keep the skin tone youthful.

Turn your body into a calorie burning furnace!

Well, not quite, but walking is a great way to boost your metabolism as lots of muscles are fired into action – from tiny ones in your feet, to your legs, your central core and, if you are walking properly, your upper body too. So walking briskly is a good way to expend energy. What's more, your metabolism will remain raised a fraction so that you get a slight 'afterburn' effect – which means that you will continue to burn calories after you have put your feet up!

A quick word about metabolism

Even while we are sleeping, there are involuntary processes going on in our bodies that require energy – breathing, cell renewal and digestion to name just a few. The amount of energy we require for these life processes is called the basal metabolic rate (BMR). Taking exercise, like walking, will increase your calorie requirements over and above your BMR, not only during exercise but for some time afterwards, depending on the intensity, hence the term 'boosting your metabolism'.

Can you increase your BMR?

Yes you can! A person's BMR is determined by several factors including gender, weight and age, but you can have some influence over it. Our body composition (the proportion of fat to lean muscle we have) has a direct effect on our metabolism. Muscle tissue is metabolically pretty active, which means it requires a constant source of energy to maintain it even while we are sleeping. So the more muscle you have, the more calories your body is able to burn 24 hours a day, 7 days a week. In addition to this, regular aerobic exercise makes our bodies more efficient at using stored fat for energy and, even better, the fat that you do eat is less likely to be stored as body fat under the skin.

Did you know?

500 grams of body fat is equivalent to 3,500 calories. If a 70-kilogram woman walks for 3.25 kilometres at any speed she would burn 186 calories. If she did that 5 days a week for a year, she would burn 48,360 calories. That's equivalent to just over 6 kilograms of body fat! This assumes that her diet remains the same and that she doesn't have too many days off. The good thing is that the 3.25 kilometres can easily be broken up into either two shorter walks or even spread out over an entire day. Using a pedometer (see page 33) to count your steps can help you to achieve similar results by making some small adjustments to your daily routine, such as parking the car in the far corner of the supermarket car park or walking up the stairs instead of taking the elevator.

Other reasons to look after your metabolism

Of course, many of us would like to lose a few pounds to boost our confidence, but on a more serious note, being overweight is a risk factor for many health conditions such as diabetes, heart disease, strokes and some cancers – particularly colon, lung and breast.

What is diabetes?

Diabetes is a metabolic disorder where the body doesn't produce enough of a hormone called insulin, which is responsible for helping turn the carbohydrate that we eat into usable energy. This results in high levels of sugar accumulating in the bloodstream. The long term effects of high blood sugar are heart disease, kidney and nerve damage and eye problems. Being overweight is a major risk factor for developing diabetes.

Type 1 diabetes is where the body produces no insulin at all and injections of the hormone are used to help regulate blood sugar levels. This disease can develop at any age, but is most commonly diagnosed in those under 20 years of age.

Type 2 diabetes is much more common than Type 1. Again, it can develop at any age, although it used to be uncommon in people under the age of 40. However, our sedentary lifestyles and increasingly poor diet means that not only are more people being diagnosed with Type 2 diabetes but the average age of people affected is getting younger. With Type 2 diabetes the body doesn't make enough insulin and what is produced is ineffective because the cells become insulin-resistant. Exercise can help regulate blood sugar levels by making the cells in the body less resistant to insulin and encouraging the muscles to take and use the sugar for energy. The good news is that these positive benefits occur almost immediately. So regular exercise not only helps to prevent Type 2 diabetes, it can also be used as a way to manage the condition once it is diagnosed.

Step-by-step to healthy muscles and joints

Walking is a weight-bearing yet low impact exercise, so it's a great way to strengthen many of the major muscle groups in the body without putting undue strain on the joints. Weight-bearing activities, like walking, stimulate the muscles' support system, i.e. the bones, ligaments and tendons, so that they become stronger too. This is especially important for the bones, because with inactivity and advancing age they begin to lose density causing them to become brittle and less resilient. This condition is known as osteoporosis and means that the bones are much more vulnerable to fracture, for example in the event of a fall. This is a condition that affects men and women, although it is more common in women, particularly after the menopause. So get walking to keep those bones strong!

If you still need convincing

- Strong muscles look better and give you confidence.
- Stronger muscles tire less easily and do a better job of stabilizing the joints involved in walking, such as ankles, knees and hips.
- Muscles provide storage for an important amino acid called glutamine which is necessary for a healthy immune system. The more muscle mass you have the more glutamine you can store.

To get the most health benefits from walking you really need to assess other areas of your lifestyle too, such as diet (see Chapter 8), stress levels, smoking and sleep, so that you are looking at the whole picture.

Emotional benefits

Walk yourself happy!

> 'In every walk with nature one receives far
> more than he seeks.'
> **John Muir**

There are so many ways that going for even a gentle walk can make us happier. Aerobic exercise releases 'feelgood' chemicals called endorphins into the bloodstream and has been shown to help in the treatment of mild depression. This feelgood factor is increased significantly if you walk somewhere pleasant, for example in woods or by a river. Walking with a friend or as part of an organized group adds a social element and is a good way to catch up with people as well as providing extra security. Being happy can help you in all sorts of areas of your life. It might be that you sleep better, are calmer at work or less likely to crave that bar of chocolate.

Reduce stress

The feelgood factor reaches further than simply putting a smile on your face though, it helps you to relax and therefore reduces stress. Stress can be the root cause of all sorts of problems, from a weak immune system, poor sleep patterns, lack of libido, digestion problems and more serious conditions like high blood pressure, which is a risk factor associated with heart disease.

Increase clarity and confidence

Many people experience heightened mental clarity and confidence when out walking, which provides a chance to view problems from a more positive perspective. Others also find their creativity is sparked during a walk.

> 'Above all do not lose your desire to walk. Every day I walk myself into a state of well-being and walk away from every illness. I have walked myself into my best thoughts and I know of no thought so burdensome that one cannot walk away from it. But by sitting still, and the more one sits still, the closer one comes to feeling ill... if one keeps on walking everything will be alright.'
> **Sean Kierkegaard**

Types of walking

Broadly speaking, walking falls into five different categories. If you are reading this book, it seems highly likely that you are looking to increase your fitness. Obviously your current fitness level, which we'll come on to in Chapter 2, is going to dictate where on this scale you are likely to start, but the beauty of walking is that by varying the intensity to suit you, there is no reason why you can't take a walk in the hills, join a rambling club or even enter a walking event.

Ambling or strolling

This is walking at it's most relaxed. It is an unhurried pace and you should be able to talk normally to whoever you are with and generally take time to enjoy the surroundings. Because walking at this pace does not particularly challenge the cardiovascular system (the heart and lungs) it may not increase your fitness significantly but can still be useful as part of a weight-loss programme as you will be burning calories over and above your BMR. This type of walking is also a good way to reduce stress, which is always beneficial.

Rambling

This takes place in the countryside in organized groups who are often members of the Ramblers Association (see page 125). Walks take place on bridle-paths, national trails, footpaths and in national parks. The pace and terrain can vary considerably but rambling is a good way to see the countryside and include a social element. The walking is more likely to be on an uneven surface which is beneficial as it increases the workload of the stabilizing muscles which can get lazy if we always walk on flat, predictable surfaces.

Hill- and fell-walking

As the name suggests, this type of walking takes you up and down hills. Walking uphill, quite often on uneven surfaces, increases the amount of work the muscles must do so this can be a really challenging exercise session. Even walking downhill is harder than walking on the flat. Of course the terrain and pace will dictate intensity to a degree, but if you are a complete beginner it may be wise to stick to flatter courses initially.

Powerwalking

Powerwalking or 'fitness walking' is done at a brisk positive pace. The speed is dictated to a certain extent by current fitness levels – it can range from the kind of pace that we walk at when late for an appointment, to almost as fast as jogging pace. This kind of walking challenges the cardiovascular system and really impacts on fitness levels, bringing with it all the associated benefits.

Racewalking

Racewalking is an Olympic event and has a characteristic technique. Walkers are watched very closely while racing because at the speeds involved it is very easy to break into what could technically be classed as a run, which leads to disqualification. Once again though, at the other end of the scale, thousands of people each year enter walking events either to raise money or to reach a goal they have set themselves, and while it may be a 'race' they are not walking very fast.

CHAPTER 2
HOW FIT ARE YOU?

In order to measure the results of an exercise programme you need to know your fitness level before you begin and what your aims are, so that you can set yourself realistic goals, both short and long term. On the following pages you will find a series of basic fitness tests that you can do yourself. You should do all of the tests and record your results. The purpose of this is that the results will help you choose which walking programme (see page 47) is most suitable for you and once you have followed the programme for a few weeks you can retest yourself and monitor your improvements. Retest yourself every three months or so and compare your results.

Note that this is a very basic range of tests. If you feel concerned about your current fitness level you should consult your doctor or have a more thorough assessment from a fitness professional. If you don't like the idea of going to a gym for this, find out about personal trainers in your area as many are able to conduct a full fitness appraisal at your home. This will usually include a blood pressure check and lung function assessment, as well as body composition and flexibility tests.

Health and fitness safety-first checklist

Generally, walking is a very safe form of exercise but if you answer 'yes' to any of the questions below, or if you have any other conditions or concerns, you should consult your GP before starting any sort of exercise programme.

Are you currently being treated for high blood pressure?

Are you diabetic?

Do you have arthritis or other joint problems, e.g. knees, ankles?

Do you have rheumatoid arthritis?

Have you broken any bones recently?

Have you had or do you have heart disease or other heart-related conditions?

Do you have any history of an irregular heartbeat?

Do you ever suffer from episodes of dizziness or palpitations?

*Do you ever experience pains or feelings of tightness
in your chest?*

*Have you had or do you have any heart infections
as a result of a virus?*

Are you asthmatic?

Are you epileptic?

Are you pregnant?

Do you smoke?

Are you very overweight, with a BMI over 30? (See opposite.)

Are you recovering from a heart attack or stroke?

Do you suffer from migraine headaches?

Are you on medication?

Are you recovering from surgery?

Body measurements

Weight

Make a note of whether you weigh yourself with shoes on or off etc., so that you weigh yourself in the same way each time. Keeping track of your weight can be very motivating if you are hitting your goals, but try not to worry if the scales aren't always friendly! Remember that muscle is more dense than fat and it is possible that you lose some body fat and put on some lean muscle tissue through your walking, especially if you are new to exercise. More muscle burns more calories so, assuming you eat the same, you should find that over time you start to lose weight. If you think about it, gaining weight usually happens quite gradually over a period of months or years so it's unrealistic to expect it to melt away in the first couple of weeks!

Body mass index (BMI)

Your BMI is the relationship between your weight and height and can be used to determine your risk of developing conditions related to being either under- or over-weight. For example, having a BMI of less than 18.5 carries a risk of osteoporosis while having a BMI over 30 indicates a greater risk of cardiovascular disease and diabetes.

BMI	
Less than 18.5	underweight
18.5–24.9	ideal
25–29.9	overweight
30–39.9	obese
40+	very obese

How do I calculate my BMI?

A fairly simple way to find your BMI is to use one of the many Internet calculators available (see Useful resources, page 125). Or use the following calculation: measure your height in metres and square it; divide your weight by your squared height. Here's an example for a person who is 1.65 metres tall and weighs 65 kilograms.

Calculation
1.65 x 1.65 = 2.72
65 ÷ 2.72 = 23.8

The BMI of this person is 23.8.

Waist/hip ratio

This is a useful and straightforward test which will give you a good idea as to how your body fat is distributed. This is important because research has shown that people who carry more body fat around their waist, i.e. 'apple-shaped', have a higher risk of heart disease. Those who carry their body fat mostly around the hip area, i.e. 'pear-shaped', tend to be healthier.

How do I calculate my waist/hip ratio?

Measure round your waist at the narrowest point and then around your hips at the widest point making sure that the tape measure is the same level all the way round. Then divide the waist measurement by the hip measurement. The result is your waist/hip ratio.

Waist/hip ratio		
Men	Women	Health Risk
Less than 0.86	*Less than 0.74*	*Low*
0.86–0.92	*0.74–0.8*	*Moderate*
0.92–1.0	*0.8–0.86*	*High*
Greater than 1.0	*Greater than 0.86*	*Very high*

Cardiovascular fitness

Resting heart rate

This is a good indicator as to how efficient your heart is. See page 8 to find out how to check your resting heart rate. It is influenced by how fit you are and, to a certain degree, genetics. Generally, the lower the resting heart rate, the stronger and more efficient the heart is. The average resting heart rate for an adult is 72 beats per minute (bpm). Anything lower than this is a bonus, but if it is higher than 85 bpm you need to get walking! The good news is that it should come down as you get fitter.

Did you know?
It is not unusual for a trained endurance athlete to have a resting heart rate in the 30s.

One-mile walk test

What do I need for this?

You need a reasonably flat, level one-mile course. Measure the course by cycling, if you have a mileometer on your bike, driving in your car, or by using an Ordnance Survey® map. Make a note of the route, including the start and finish points so that you remember for next time. Unless you have a heart rate monitor, take a digital watch with you as you will need to be able to find your pulse fairly quickly when you finish the mile. Your heart rate will drop quite quickly when you stop walking, particularly if you are already reasonably fit, so speed here is important. You should also use the digital watch to time your mile accurately.

How do I do it?

Walk the mile course as fast as you can and when you reach the finish, note the time it took and find your pulse. Count the number of beats in 10 seconds and multiply this by 6 to give you your finish heart rate. If you find that you can't walk the entire mile (due to shortness of breath, pain etc.), make a note of how many minutes you walked for before you stopped so that next time you can try to walk a little longer.

Why should I do it?

The aim of this exercise is to give you a starting point. You will have walked 1 mile and recorded your time and heart rate at the finish. When you come back and retest yourself, in say 3-months time, you can compare your results. In an ideal world if your walk took the same time during your retest you should find that your heart rate at the end was a little lower. Or perhaps your walk was a little quicker and your heart rate was lower, both indicators that you are fitter. However, you need to remember that this is just a guide. Your heart rate is totally individual to you and can also vary significantly from day to day, down to each beat. Things like humidity, fatigue, when and what you last ate, stress and time of day can all affect your heart rate during exercise, so if it doesn't behave exactly as you hoped when you retest, don't worry! The changes you are making are lifelong, so over a period of months you will get fitter and your heart rate will respond but the adaptations to exercise take time. What you should also notice is that everyday tasks feel easier and that you have more energy and generally feel better in yourself.

Core strength

Almost all the movements that we make originate from our core, or in the words of Joseph Pilates, our 'girdle of strength'. It comprises the shoulder and pelvic areas, most of the torso actually. In the shoulder area, muscles attach from the collarbones and shoulder blades into the back and are responsible for stabilizing important joints, such as the shoulder, so that it doesn't dislocate when challenged. Likewise, abdominal, spinal and gluteal (bottom) muscles attach to the pelvis, keeping it in the right place in relation to the spine. Think of these muscles like guide-ropes on a tent. If all the ropes are the optimum length and tension, the tent stays up (if you're lucky!). However, if some of the ropes are very short and tight, and others are too long and a little loose, your tent is shaky. The same principal applies to the body and quite often imbalanced or weak core muscles lead to poor posture and lower back pain (see page 38). Core strength is key to stabilizing your body while walking.

Core strength and walking

Good core strength will:

- *Help to maintain good posture.*

- *Reduce fatigue and therefore the chances of injury.*

- *Provide support to the lower back.*

The plank*

No you don't have to walk it! 'The plank' is a yoga-based exercise and an excellent measure of core strength. It is also a very effective tummy-flattening exercise in its own right and who wouldn't welcome that? Don't hold your breath while holding the half plank or plank position.

1 Lie face down on a mat, resting on your elbows.

2 Lift your hips so that you are resting on your knees, taking care to maintain a neutral spine position (see page 39).

3 Pull your navel towards your spine to support your back. This is a half-plank.

4 For a full plank, come up on to your toes.

Have a practice first and then time yourself for 20 seconds in either a half or full plank. If you are not able to maintain the position for the 20-second duration, note how long you lasted and try to improve on that next time. A good aim is to try and increase the time by 5 seconds each time you retest. If you can hold either a half or full plank for 1 minute, maintaining perfect posture, then your core strength is excellent.

*NOTE: If you have any problems with your back or if you have high blood pressure then omit this test.

Flexibility

Flexibility determines the range of movement at different joints in the bodies. Very tight muscles can be more susceptible to injury so it is a good idea to include some basic stretching exercises in your walking programme (see page 47). The 'Sit and reach' test below will give you an idea as to the flexibility of your lower back and hamstrings. Tight hamstrings can have implications for lower back problems so it is a good idea to try and keep them supple. We also tend to lose some flexibility in our muscles as we get older – it comes down to the simple adage 'if you don't use it you lose it!' But the good news is that no matter how inflexible you are it can always be improved with some well-chosen stretches – it's never too late to start.

Sit and reach test

1 Sit with your back against a wall with your legs straight out in front of you.

2 Place one hand on top of the other, resting them on your thighs. Reach forward with your arms, down your legs, as far as you comfortably can. Try not to 'bounce' into the stretch and make sure that you don't allow your knees to come up. Where are you reaching to?

Flexibility	
I find it hard to even sit in the start position!	*Very poor*
I can reach my thighs	*Poor*
I can reach my knees and upper shins	*Fair*
I can reach my lower shins/ankles	*Good*
I can reach my toes and further	*Excellent*

Balance

As with flexibility, we lose our sense of balance, particularly with increasing age, if it is not challenged on a daily basis. Good balance relies on our brains sending the right messages to stimulate our muscles and our flexibility. Lack of balance is often the reason for falling as we get older and with that comes the increased risk of broken bones, so maintaining good balance is important. Try the test below and see how you get on. Don't worry if you don't have good balance as it is something you can work on. Walking will improve your sense of balance, especially if you walk on uneven surfaces and practise standing on one leg for basic activities such as cleaning your teeth.

One leg standing

You will need a stopwatch or someone to time you – or catch you!

1 Stand with both arms down by your side and lift one knee so that you are standing on one leg. Try to pull your tummy button in towards your spine slightly as you do this to engage your core muscles and help you balance.

2 Time yourself to see how long you can stay on each leg.

TIME	RATING
1 second or less	Very poor
2–3 seconds	Poor
4–6 seconds	Fair
7–9 seconds	Good
10 seconds or more	Excellent

What are your goals?

'If it isn't happening, make it happen.'
David Hemmings

By choosing to read this book you have already shown that you would like to make some changes in your life by starting a walking programme. You have established how fit you are by working through the tests on the previous pages or having a fitness assessment with a personal trainer. The next thing to do is decide what your long- and short-term goals are and how you are going to achieve them.

This is going to provide you with the impetus to really go for it. Your goals do not necessarily have to be all walking-based and in fact it is better to take a holistic view and look at other areas of your life that you could also improve on. Think 'SMARTER' when deciding what your goals may be.

S   Specific
M   Measurable
A   Agreed
R   Realistic
T   Time limit
E   Exciting and enjoyable
R   Record your results and reward

Be specific

If your long-term goal is to lose weight, decide how much weight. If it is to walk faster, how much faster? If you would like to enter a walking event, which event will it be and when? Do not be vague about what it is that you want to achieve.

Make your goal measurable

Otherwise how will you know if you are achieving your goals? Your long-term goal might be to beat depression by starting a walking programme. Is this measurable? It can be. You could devise a scale so that you can quantify how good or how bad you are feeling on a particular day or for longer periods, say a week or a month. Then you can look at previous months to see if there is a general improvement.

Agree your goal

In other words, tell someone else about your goal as it will 'firm up' your commitment to it. You could write your goal down on a piece of paper and place it where you will see it often, such as the fridge door, (a particularly good place if your aim is to lose weight!) as this will continually reinforce it.

Realistic

This is tricky. Some people say that your goals must be realistic for you to attain them, otherwise ultimately your motivation will suffer and you will give up trying. Others, and I am one of them, would argue that sometimes we don't know what we are capable of until we try!

'Shoot for the moon.
Even if you miss, you'll land among the stars.'
Brian Littrell

Perhaps you are unable to walk one mile at the present time as you are overweight and have not exercised for 15 years. Your aim might be to walk across the Gobi Desert in a year's time. To some this may seem an unrealistic goal, but if you break this down into weekly or monthly goals that you know you can achieve, it can be very motivating. You may need to wait for another year until you achieve your main goal, you might even change your mind about your goal altogether and settle for walking a marathon instead, but that is still 25 miles further than the 1 mile you struggled to complete when you set out. So, be realistic in the short term but do not underestimate yourself and what you can achieve if you set your mind to it!

Time limit

If you have set yourself a really challenging goal it may take you longer to achieve it than you first thought. However, if you break your goal down into monthly short-term aims you can be reasonably realistic about timings. This will stop you falling into the trap of 'I'll start tomorrow', because tomorrow can sometimes go on for a long time! If you are losing weight, set yourself small, attainable weekly or fortnightly targets. If you hit each one you will slowly but surely lose the weight, which is the healthiest and best way to keep it off. If you cannot walk a mile at the moment give yourself a month to do it. This will give you the motivation to get up and go, even when the weather is not being kind.

Exciting and enjoyable

Whatever your goal, the process which takes you there needs to be enjoyable or you will not succeed. For walking-related goals, try different routes. If you usually walk in town, take a trip out to the countryside or the beach and take advantage of different sights and sounds, or perhaps even visit another country. There are plenty of walking-based holidays available now with experienced guides and great routes. Arrange to meet friends or family somewhere or join a walking group to make your walking a more social activity.

Record your results and reward!

It is well worth keeping a 'walking diary' so that you can track your progress (see the example on page 113). It is something for you to refer back to when you are looking for improvements.

If you reach your goals make sure you reward yourself!

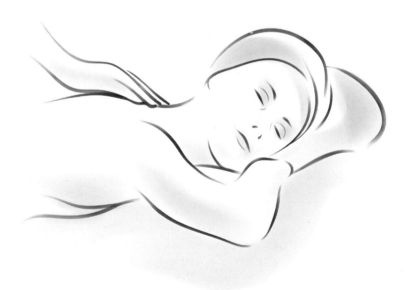

CHAPTER 3
GET EQUIPPED

The equipment you need to start walking for fitness is minimal. However, as with any sports activity, there are plenty of gadgets available to buy if you wish.

Items you need:
- Good shoes and socks

- Comfortable clothing suitable for different conditions

- Water bottle

Items that may be useful:
- Pedometer

- Heart rate monitor

- Bum bag

- Basic first-aid kit

- Mobile phone and/or personal alarm

Love your feet

Our feet are intricate structures that have to work incredibly hard. The average person walks around 177,000 kilometres during a lifetime which is a lot of steps, particularly when you consider that we don't always wear shoes that are kind to our feet!

Did you know?
Your feet comprise: 26 bones – which take from birth to 18 years of age to harden and make up a quarter of all the bones in your body, 33 joints, 107 ligaments and 19 muscles.

Are all feet the same?

If only it were that simple. All the little joints in the feet are designed to make them flexible so that they can walk over uneven surfaces. Together with muscles, ligaments and tendons, these joints also form an arch in the foot so that it can support our body weight and more, when performing our daily activities. Or at least that's what should happen. In reality, the biomechanics of each and every one of our skeletons is complicated and sometimes joints don't align quite as they should. This causes compensations to occur elsewhere in the body which may or may not cause problems. In our feet there are two compensations to be aware of when choosing your footwear, and this is important for all your shoes, not just those that you will be using for your exercise sessions.

To find out more about your feet, wet them and stand on a piece of card or on a floor surface which shows up your footprints. Compare your print to the diagrams below.

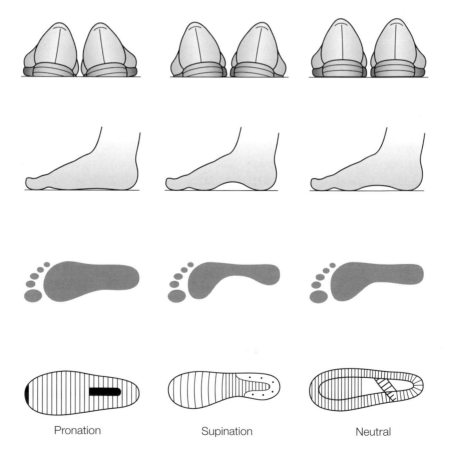

| Pronation | Supination | Neutral |

Pronation

This is a really common occurrence and one that many people aren't even aware of. When the foot pronates it rolls inwards and flattens the sole of the foot so that the arch becomes smaller or disappears completely. It means that the foot can't bear weight as efficiently and that the structures within the foot are moving around more than they should which can cause discomfort.

How do I know if I pronate?
There are a couple ways you can spot this.

1 Compare your print to the diagrams on page 26. If the whole of your foot is in contact with the floor, then you are overpronating.

2 Look at your existing shoes. Place them on a flat surface and look at the heel end. If they are falling towards each other slightly, that is if they have worn on the insides quicker than the outsides, the chances are that you are overpronating. Training shoes are particularly good for showing this up. Look at page 26 to make a comparison. You can also have a look at the soles of the shoes to see how the treads are wearing.

Best shoes for pronators?
If you are pronating then you need extra support along the inner edge of your foot. Shoes which are made on a straight last (mould) will give more support to this area, which is important because if you overpronate you will place more stress on other structures in your lower body, such as your knees and hips. If you pronate severely it may be advisable to see a chiropodist or podiatrist who will be able to assess your feet in more detail and may suggest using orthotics (specialist moulded inserts) to provide support in the right places.

Supination

This will show itself as a particularly high arch. The joints of the foot are less flexible and this rigidity means that its shock-absorbing abilities are reduced.

How do I know if I supinate?
1 Compare your print to the diagrams on page 26. If you supinate you won't see much of your mid-foot in the print. Instead you will see the ball of your foot, toes and heel.

2 Look also at your existing shoes. Place them on a level surface and look at the heel end. They will lean away from each other if you supinate. You can also check the treads to see if the outside is wearing quicker than the inside.

Best shoes for supinators?
Because the shock-absorbing abilities of the foot are compromised, a shoe that offers good cushioning in the mid-foot area is important for people who supinate. Also look for shoes which, if you look at their soles, have a curved shape (see page 26). It may be a good idea to see a chiropodist or podiatrist for further advice.

Neutral

1 Compare your print to the diagrams on page 26. If you have a neutral foot you will have a slight arch in the mid-foot area and your wet footprint will show your heel, a small area of your mid-foot, the balls of your feet and your toes. This indicates that you have just the right amount of pronation and supination.

2 Place your existing shoes on a level surface. They should be neither falling into each other or leaning away and if you look underneath at the soles the wear should be even on both sides.

Best shoes for a neutral foot?
You are in the happy position that you will feel quite at home in most shapes and styles, although they will obviously need to be good quality shoes suitable for walking.

What type of shoe is best for walking?

Now that you have established what foot type you have, you need to choose your shoes. Ultimately this depends where you are likely to be walking and what type of walking you will be doing. Clearly if you are powerwalking on pavements you are going to need different shoes to someone who hikes on coastal paths.

Ideal walking shoe This will probably look like a normal trainer and will cover most needs unless you want to climb a mountain, in which case you have probably bought the wrong book!

Running shoes These are a suitable option in the absence of walking shoes and if they meet the criteria listed in the box on page 29.

Off-road shoes Fairly good if you are walking on tracks or uneven terrain as they have deeper treads that offer a better grip. The downside is that because they are more rigid they are usually much less flexible so they can be tiring for the feet over long distances.

Crosstraining shoes Not advisable. As the name suggests, they are designed to be used across a range of activities and tend to be quite rigid as a result.

Hiking boots If you are going to be on a one-off walk on very rugged terrain then well-fitting hiking boots are supportive and protective from the elements. They are not really compatible with walking briskly as they don't flex easily and can be quite heavy.

What to look for in a walking shoe

Flexibility A walking shoe actually needs to be more flexible than a running shoe as a walker's foot flexes more. Don't be afraid to pick up different shoes and 'feel' how flexible they are.

Stability Does the shoe have good arch support? Also go for shoes with lower heels, no more than 2.5 centimetres higher than the rest of the sole or you may end up with sore shins. Heels with a slight flare, or a 'positive' heel are also not a good idea for fitness walking as they tend to encourage a forward-leaning posture which can put more stress through the hips and knees. Instead, look for shoes with a 'negative' heel, i.e. slightly rounded, such as the shoes made by Masai Barefoot Technology® (MBT). These will encourage you to walk with an upright posture taking stress away from the lower back, hips, knees and shins.

Shock absorbers Make sure the shoes provide good cushioning so they absorb some of the shock while you are walking, especially if you are likely to be walking on pavements or hard surfaces most of the time. Check for this in the heel and the ball of the foot area.

Laces It's important that your heel doesn't slip and stays put in your shoe to prevent your foot slipping forward and laces are a good way of ensuring this.

A perfect fit The most important aspect of all! Ideally, find a specialist sports shoe shop as they will be able to give you a thorough fitting with lots of advice along the way, such as how to lace your shoes for a narrow or wide fit. They will be able to tell you what kind of shoe will best serve your needs and may have a treadmill so that you can try them out before you buy. Don't forget to take the socks you are going to wear with your walking shoes and try to go for a fitting towards the end of the day when your feet will be slightly bigger.

Fitting points

- *Make sure you have room between your longest toe, usually the big toe, and the end of the shoe. This can be up to 1 centimetre but no more otherwise your feet will move around in them too much which may cause blisters.*

- *The shoe needs to have enough depth so that the tops of your toes aren't pressed against the upper as this will make them sore.*

- *You need enough width for your toes to sit comfortably or you run the risk of getting blisters.*

- *Check inside the shoe to make sure there are no rough areas or seams that are too prominent.*

How long will they last?

As part of your walking diary (see page 115) you will be noting how many kilometres/ miles you are walking. Ideally you should replace your walking shoes every 560–800 kilometres as the support inside the shoe will start to weaken leaving your feet more vulnerable. Try to keep your walking shoes just for your walking sessions so that you know how far they have been and no matter how dirty they get, don't put them in the washing machine as this too will weaken the support inside the shoe.

Clothing

Socks

Although you may feel you have plenty of socks already, it's definitely worth investing in a few pairs of good sports socks for your walking. They are likely to be made from quick-drying synthetic fibres, such as CoolMax®, rather than natural materials such as wool or cotton which don't dry easily and can cause blisters and soreness. They may also have anti-microbial properties to combat odour – something to think about in the warmer months.

Thicker socks are usually a better bet than thinner ones as they often have extra cushioning at the ball of the foot and heel areas, although this is a matter of personal preference. Some people find they feel a little 'bumpy' and prefer a smoother, lighter sock. The very short trainer liner-type sock may be alright if you are used to them, but be aware that they can slip down into your shoes and don't offer your Achilles tendon much protection.

Some people also swear by anti-blister socks which are made of two layers that rub against each other instead of you.

Back to basics – underwear

Try to avoid cotton underwear as it doesn't wick moisture well, so if it gets damp through either perspiration or rain it will stay damp, which can feel really unpleasant next to your skin, not to mention cold in the winter. In periods of really cold weather you may want to consider long-sleeved vests and 'long johns' made from synthetic, lightweight fibres – they are excellent at keeping the moisture away from your skin and will help to keep you snug and dry.

Sports bras

Bras have come a long way since 1893 when Marie Tucek patented the first 'breast supporter' which is the earliest known design to bear any resemblance to our modern-day bra. It has been shown that up to 56 per cent of women experience breast pain during exercise. This is because breasts are largely composed of fatty tissue with very little in the way of support. The breasts are interlaced with structures called 'Coopers ligaments' which offer some support, but these stretch easily with exercise, particularly as impact increases. So a couple of good sports bras that fit well are an important addition to any woman's walking wardrobe.

———— What should you look for in a sports bra? ————

• A snug fit, but not so tight that it digs in or makes breathing tricky!

• Good support from moulded cups. If you have larger breasts you should go for this type of bra rather than the cropped top-style bras which tend to simply compress the breasts and don't offer as much support.

• Comfy straps that are wide but don't cut into your shoulders. They also need to be non-stretchy to maximize support. Bras with a racer-style back in a 'Y' shape are also more supportive, as are ones that fasten at the back rather than the front.

• Fabric should be breathable which will be much more comfortable next to your skin and help to keep you dry, which means you should avoid cotton. Be aware that any fabric will age with repeated wearing and washing, so you will

Outerwear

The main objective is to be as comfortable as possible during your walks otherwise you'll be heading home before you planned! Some points to consider:

If it's hot
Your first consideration should be to try and walk either before 11am or after 3pm so that you don't overexpose yourself to the sun which is at its hottest between these times. Outside of these hours it may still be warm so go for vests and T-shirts made from wicking fabrics, such as CoolMax®, which will take moisture from your skin to the outside of the garment where it can evaporate. Some of these fabrics are so light you could even wear a long-sleeved top to give you extra protection from the sun. Whatever you wear on your bottom half you need to make sure that seams and excess fabric are kept to a minimum as these can cause chafing on the insides of your thighs. Cotton-Lycra® cycling shorts and leggings are great from this point of view although not popular with everyone (they don't leave very much to the imagination!). When buying your shorts make sure they are long enough so that they don't 'ride' up your thighs, which can be irritating.

A baseball-style cap to protect your scalp and a pair of sunglasses are useful additions when it's hot, along with some sunscreen.

If it's cold
Layering is the key. Pick a long-sleeved vest-type top and/or leggings in a technical wicking fibre to go next to your skin as your base layer. This will help to keep you warm and dry. Then add layers depending on how cold it is. Fleecy tops can be useful, as can a jacket. You can buy these either as one jacket where the fleece zips inside the outer water-repellent layer or purchase them separately. Make sure fabrics are breathable as well as being water-resistant – you don't want to end up like a 'boil in the bag' meal! Remember too that if you wear layers you can always remove something and tie it around your waist if you get too hot. Better that than being cold. Lightweight hat, gloves and maybe a scarf will also help when it's chilly outside.

Gadgets

Pedometers

As with most gadgets you can spend as much or as little as you want on a pedometer. They are small devices that count your steps and are clipped on to your waistband or the strap of a bum bag. Once you input your step length, a pedometer can calculate the distance you have walked as well as other data such as calorie expenditure and speed. Some pedometers have other useful features, for example a stopwatch or panic alarm, so it's worth shopping around. Simplicity is often the best way to go as there is less to go wrong and less reading of instruction manuals. However, if you really want lots of functions you can buy pedometers with radios, ones that will speak to you and others enable you to upload the details of your walking session to your computer.

Global Positioning Systems (GPS)

These are battery-operated devices, small enough to fit into a bum bag or pocket. They use satellite signals to determine where you are and how fast you are travelling, and are really a very advanced compass, so they are useful if you are in unfamiliar territory and your map-reading skills aren't great. If you have set routes and know where you are going it is probably a gadget you can do without as they are quite expensive compared to a pedometer. They also have a limited battery life which can be a little annoying if it runs out during a walk.

Do I need a pedometer?

A pedometer is by no means a necessity. Some of the walking programmes later in the book have been designed around the use of one, but there are other programmes where a pedometer isn't necessary. It can be very motivating for individuals to see how many calories they have burnt or the fact that they are covering more steps in the same period of time. They are also a great way of actually measuring how much you do. For example, it is recommended that we take 10,000 steps each day, so if you wear your pedometer for a day and find that you are only covering 4,000 steps you can aim to increase the number of steps by 500 per day that week, then another 500 the week after, until you reach the magic number. You'll be surprised how many extra steps you can notch up just parking in the far corner of the supermarket car park! A very basic pedometer really isn't expensive, so I'd recommend that if you're going to take your fitness walking seriously, you should buy one.

Are they accurate?

Inside your pedometer is a small pendulum-type device which is motion sensitive and is triggered with each step you take. For this device to work properly, and therefore accurately, the pedometer needs to be parallel to the ground, so make sure that it sits level on your waistband. For the same reason pedometers work most accurately on flat terrain. Remember too, that if you are using your pedometer to calculate calorie consumption, the totals will be just a guide. A pedometer only counts steps, it doesn't know whether they were taken on the flat or walking up Mount Everest! Obviously you would burn significantly more calories walking up the latter!

Check your pedometer

If you suspect that your pedometer is inaccurate, walk a known distance and see if it agrees. Bear in mind though, that there will always be slight variations as the pedometer calculates distance travelled on your stride length and this will not always be the same.

What's the best way to measure step or stride length?

When you first get your pedometer read the instructions that come with it to establish whether it requires you to enter your step length or your stride length. Step length is the distance between the heel of one foot and the heel of the other. Stride length is the distance between the heel strike of the right foot to the next heel strike of the right foot; in other words, two steps. Most pedometers will ask you for your step length but you do need to check. There are lots of different ways to measure your step length but one of the easiest is to measure a distance of say 10 metres and mark the beginning and end clearly. Walk the 10 metres and count your steps. Divide 10 metres by the number of steps you took. Try to walk in a relaxed way, without over-exaggerating. This will make your pedometer information more accurate.

Heart rate monitors

A heart rate monitor is a good way of measuring the intensity of your walking session. Most heart rate monitors comprise a chest strap and watch. The chest strap picks up electrical signals from your heart and transmits them to the watch that will then display your heart rate in beats per minute.

Are they expensive?

They can be! You can buy a basic heart rate monitor that just displays the heart rate for a small outlay, whereas a top of the range monitor could be a more significant purchase. Useful features can include a stopwatch, upper and lower heart rate warning sounds for if your heart rate goes higher or lower than your desired level, calorie consumption, time of day and date, computer download options and even a 'foot pod'. This is a small device which attaches to your walking shoe and can relay information back regarding your pace and distance travelled. Whether you need all this data is something only you can decide!

Do I really need one?
You don't need a heart rate monitor to go out for a walk but that said, if you do have one it can take some of the guesswork out of your walking sessions. If you follow one of the programmes in this book that is based on intensity of workout for example, you will know whether you are achieving the desired level just by glancing at your watch. If your heart rate is too low, you will need to increase the pace a little and if it is too high you can slow down, safe in the knowledge that you are working hard enough. If you don't want to invest in a heart rate monitor there are other ways that you can monitor intensity (see page 48).

Other items

Water bottle
Even in winter you should carry a bottle of water with you if you plan to be out for longer than 30 minutes. You can buy plastic or light metal sports bottles with special drinking tops to minimize spillages and they often come in ergonomic designs so that they are easy to grip. If you prefer not to hold your water you can buy bum bags with built in water holders.

Bum bags
These are not very big and once you get used to wearing one you will hardly notice it. Use them to hold any or all of the following items as appropriate to the circumstances in which you are walking:

- Keys

- Water

- Mobile phone (make sure emergency phone numbers are in your phone book)

- Small amount of money

- Snack – such as a piece of fruit or a cereal bar

- Lip salve

- Sunscreen

- Sunglasses

- Basic first-aid items such as plasters, blister dressings and a small antiseptic wipe

- Personal alarm or whistle to attract attention

- Any medication you may need

- Foil blanket – you can buy these in sports shops; they do not take up much room and can be useful if you injure yourself and are immobile

Music

Opinions are divided on this issue. Some people can't live without their music while out walking and others can't imagine anything worse than not being able to hear what is going on around them. For your own safety it is not advisable, but if you do listen to music through headphones make sure the volume is low enough so that you can hear what is happening around you. If you are walking on country lanes for example, you need to be able to hear the approach of a car or someone walking up behind you.

CHAPTER 4
GETTING STARTED

So now you are equipped and ready to go, but there a few points to consider before you march out the door. Although walking is something we can all do from an early age it doesn't necessarily follow that we are good at it! If you take some time to work on your posture, technique and breathing while walking, you will reap the benefits.

Posture

What is good posture?
Good posture means that all of the joints in the body are aligned in the most efficient way possible. This applies not only to standing but sitting and lying down also.

—————————— **Benefits of good posture:** ——————————

• Well-aligned joints allow the muscles, tendons and ligaments that are attached to them to work properly with no undue strain.

• More efficient muscles don't tire so easily, resulting in you being able to walk further or faster for the same energy cost and effort.

• Joints endure less wear and tear so problems like arthritis are less likely.

• Good spinal posture can free up space for the lungs, enabling more efficient breathing.

• Less stress and strain on the spine so less chance of back pain.

• It looks and feels better!

Did you know?

It is estimated that 80 per cent of lower back pain is posture related.

Why does it feel uncomfortable when I work on my posture?

It is because muscles have a memory that means they get used to doing the same things in the same way. By changing posture even slightly, you are asking your muscles to do something they are not used to and this may feel slightly unnatural to begin with. The first step to changing your posture is becoming aware of what your posture is like right now. Have a look at the diagrams below – which one do you most resemble?

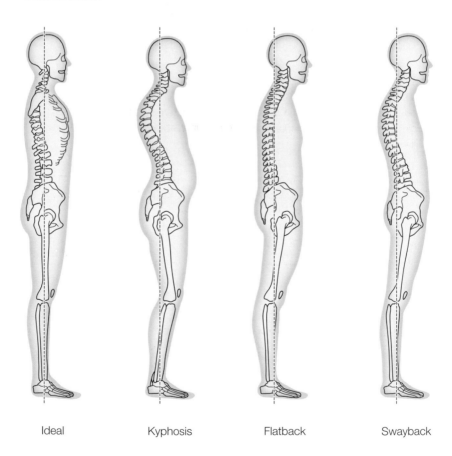

| Ideal | Kyphosis | Flatback | Swayback |

Postural awareness exercise

1 Stand side-on to a full length mirror.

2 Allow your posture to 'slump', which usually means the tummy sticks out and the shoulders come down and forward. Hopefully your posture is not usually this bad!

3 Now imagine you have a string attached to the top of your head and that it is drawing you upwards, lengthening your spine.

4 Hold your head up and tuck your chin in to your chest slightly so that the back of your neck is lengthened. You may even feel the muscles at the back of your neck, into your hairline, gently stretching at this point.

5 Draw your shoulder-blades down and back which will lengthen your neck further. Your chest should feel open.

6 Pull your tummy button in gently towards your spine. This will activate deep core muscles called the *transversus abdominis*, which are important in stabilizing your mid-section and supporting your spine. The key here is to keep it gentle – if you suck your abdominals in too far it will affect your ability to breathe 'from your belly'.

7 Tuck your buttocks In slightly, particularly if you have a large curve in your lower back. Don't tuck them in so much that you lose the curve altogether though, your spine should be in a neutral position.

8 Hold this position for at least 10 seconds, taking a few deep breaths. Notice how easy it is to breathe. You may also feel a little taller and slimmer!

9 Now relax.

Sometimes when people try to improve posture it can make them feel a little wooden. At first, concentrate on points you feel are particularly relevant to you and work on them little by little until it feels natural. When the new improved muscle memory takes over, you won't have to think about it so much and you will feel more relaxed.

What is a neutral spine?

Lie on your back on a mat. If possible, lie alongside a mirror so you can see the position of your back. Bend your knees.

1 Imagine that you are lying on damp sand. Tilt your pelvis so that your tail bone lifts up slightly, pressing your lower back gently down into the 'sand' as if making an imprint of your spine. This is an 'imprinted' position that we do not call upon for walking as there is no curve at all and it is the curves in our spine, rather like the arches in our feet, which are responsible for bearing weight and absorbing shock.

2 Now tilt your pelvis in the opposite direction, so that you can feel your tail bone pressing into the mat. You will notice that the curve in your lower spine is accentuated and you may even be able to get a fist in the space between the mat and your back. This is an 'overextension' of the lower back and puts too much pressure on the discs in your spine. This spine position is not good for walking, but erring towards it is a very common postural fault and causes a lot of sore backs.

3 Tilt the pelvis back somewhere between positions 1 and 2, until you have a gentle curve in your lower back. There should be enough room for you to just slide your hands, palms down, into the space. This is a 'neutral spine position'.

Try finding your neutral spine position while standing by just tilting your pelvis forwards and backwards. Notice what happens to your lower back and how it feels when you find neutral.

Walk the walk

If you work on maintaining correct posture you are well on the way to good walking technique. The aim here is to give you a few more points to think about while you are actually walking, however do not try to think about everything at once as you will end up walking with a body as stiff as an ironing board! Walking is actually quite a complex activity relying on lots of muscle groups working together at the same time. If you start to break it down too much you may lose the 'flow'. Just pick one or two things to work on and stick with them until things feel more natural, you can then move on to a different aspect. Apart from racewalking, which has its own distinctive technique, these points apply to all types of walking, although there are other considerations when walking up- or down- hill for example (see page 43-44).

Head up

Hold your head up and look forward. Lengthen the back of your neck and hold your chin parallel to the ground. This ensures that your cervical spine – the neck area – is in a neutral position, placing less stress on the muscles in the back of your neck and top of your shoulders. Try to focus your sight on a point about 4–5 metres (13–16 feet) ahead of you. Obviously this is easier on predictable terrain, so use your judgement here. But in general, head up and eyes ahead and not at your shoes – think 'happy' walking!

Upper body

Relax your shoulders down and back so that your chest is open. Your arms should be bent to a 90-degree angle at the elbow and your hands should be cupped slightly, as if holding a small bird that you do not want to hurt.

As you walk, allow your shoulders to rotate slightly so you twist a little from the waist. This is beneficial for your abdominal and back muscles. Your shoulders should swing in opposition to your legs – so if your right shoulder is forward, your left leg should be in the lead position. However, make sure that you do not rotate so much that your hand or arm comes over the centre of your body.

You then need to introduce a pumping action with your arms. Keeping your elbows bent to 90 degrees, swing them back and forth in front and behind you, making sure that your trail hand does not go behind your hip and that your fore hand does not go further than chest height. Keep your elbows close to your body as you walk, perhaps just brushing your clothing on the sweep through.

If you are not used to this action you may find it quite tiring. Stick with it though as you will get stronger the more you do it. You can also lower your arms intermittently to give them a break. If you have been walking for a while and you still find this difficult you may like to try some of the resistance exercises on page 61, such as push-ups on the gym ball, to strengthen your upper body.

Why do the elbows have to be bent?

• *Walking with straight arms for a long period can cause tingling sensations and even some unpleasant swelling in the hands and fingers. Walking with a bent elbow prevents this from happening.*

• *A positive 'arm pump' will enable you to really pick up the pace.*

• *Walking with your elbows bent, and using the 'arm pump' action uses 5–10 per cent more calories – every little helps if you are trying to lose weight!*

• *This position will also help to tone up muscles in your arms and shoulders.*

Mid-section

We have already established that you need to have a slight twist at the waist which is lead by the shoulders. You also need to keep thinking about drawing your tummy button in towards your spine to engage your transversus muscles that will help to support your spine as you walk. Make sure your spine is in a neutral position, which for many people this will just involve tucking the tail bone/buttocks under the hips a little (see page 39).

Lower body

As your right shoulder comes forward, the left leg also swings through, initially with a bent knee and then straightening as the heel comes down to the ground. At this point you need to make sure you are not locking your knee out straight as this places a lot of stress on the ligaments that stabilize and support it. The left heel should come down to the ground with the ankle flexed so that the toes point skyward to approximately 45 degrees. Your foot should roll from the heel through to your toes as the weight of your body passes over it.

Finally you need to actively push off your toes to carry your momentum into the next stride. The structure of your foot combined with the spring effect of your calf muscles will see you well on your way to the next step. By this time the heel of your right leg will have struck the ground and your left leg will be starting the recovery phase. Think about walking in a straight line, as if you are walking along a tightrope. Imagine walking in snow or sand making a single line of footprints – this is more efficient than 'tramline' footprints. Keep your stride length relaxed and comfortable.

Walking uphill

Walking uphill will obviously increase the intensity of your walk as you need to propel your body weight upwards as well as forwards. Large muscle groups, such as the quadriceps at the front of your legs and the gluteals in your bottom, will have to work harder, and as these muscles have a high demand for oxygen you can expect your heart rate to rise by up to 20 per cent. This is a good way to boost your fitness but make sure that you do not overdo it. If you are so out of breath that you cannot string a few words together, you should stop until you have recovered.

_____ **Tips for walking uphill** _____

- *Try to avoid hills too early in your walk as you will find them much easier to deal with once your muscles are warm.*

- *Shorten your stride.*

- *Lean into the hill slightly to maintain your balance. Do not lean too far though, or you could strain your lower back.*

- *If the hill is very steep you can zigzag your way up so that you are moving across the slope rather than up it.*

Walking downhill

You might reasonably expect that walking downhill would be a welcome break, but actually it can be quite energy-consuming. Assisted by gravity, your pace will tend to increase as you walk downhill which necessitates the need for a 'braking' action by the legs. The steeper the slope the harder this will be. There is also more impact on the hip, knee and ankle joints as you strike the ground, so be aware of this if you have problems in these areas.

- *As with walking uphill, avoid steep descents too early in your walk if possible, until your muscles have warmed up.*

- *Keep your knees soft, i.e. slightly bent.*

- *Try to keep your stride length fairly short so that you stay in control.*

- *Keep your body upright so that your weight is evenly distributed over your hips and knees.*

- *If you have hip, knee or ankle problems or if the descent is particularly steep, you may prefer to zigzag down the slope so that you are walking across it rather than straight down.*

Breathing

'Breathing control gives man strength, vitality, inspiration and magic powers.'
Chuang Tzu

Magic powers indeed, but only if we breathe properly! Many of us use only a small proportion of our available lung space, largely due to the fact that our sedentary lifestyles do not require us to breathe any deeper. Walking provides an ideal opportunity to think about your breathing and when you get it right you will feel energized and relaxed at the same time.

Breathing exercise

1 Stand, maintaining good posture, and breathe normally. What do you notice about your breathing? You will probably see your chest rising and falling gently. Try doing this in front of a mirror to help you.

2 Now breathe really deeply. What do you notice now? Your chest is probably rising and falling more noticeably, with your shoulders also moving up and down. You may also be sucking in your stomach to get as much air in as possible.

3 Now try doing the opposite. Breathe out to start. When you breathe in, instead of pulling your tummy button in and 'sucking', think about pushing your belly button

out as the air enters your lungs. Imagine this expansion moving up into your rib cage so that your ribs move up and out and your shoulders draw back a little. Now that your lungs are full, breathe out in the reverse order. So, top of the lungs first, then allow the ribs to pull back in and down (this is almost a 'squeeze') and finally draw your belly button back in, which pushes the diaphragm up and expels all the air from your lungs. This exercise is called 'belly breathing' and is a good way to fully inflate and deflate your lungs.

Breathing during walking

Your breathing should feel natural and easy. As the pace increases so will your muscles' demand for oxygen so you will find that your breathing rate quickens and you will naturally breathe a little deeper. Just be aware of how you breathe as you pick up the pace and make sure you are using the 'belly breathing' technique to get as much oxygen into your system as possible. It's amazing how just focusing on your breathing can make you feel more relaxed but at the same time energized and mentally sharper. If you find you are getting so breathless that you cannot speak you probably need to slow down a little.

Walking – frequently asked questions

Can I use weights while walking?

Some people like to use wrist and ankle weights or hold dumbbells during their walks but this is not advisable as you are more likely to injure yourself, you will not be able to walk as fast and strength gains will be minimal. The best way to increase your strength would be to supplement your walking sessions with some carefully chosen resistance exercises (see page 60).

How hard do I need to work my arms?

This really depends on the intensity you need to achieve during your walk. For example, if you are a beginner using a heart rate monitor for example, you may find that a moderate walking pace coupled with a gentle arm action is more than enough to take your heart rate up to the target. If you are very fit and used to walking, you will probably need to use a really powerful arm pump and a brisk walking pace to get your heart rate up to where it needs to be

How fast should I walk?

This is a very difficult question to answer as there are so many variables involved. It depends on your current level of fitness, the terrain and your walking technique. Remember, pace is not everything. It is more important that you are walking at the right intensity for you rather than worrying about how fast you are going. Two people can walk at the same intensity but at completely different speeds – it's all down to the circumstances of the individual. You certainly should not increase the pace until you have a good technique firmly engrained. See page 48 to learn more about how you can measure your exercise intensity.

Are treadmills OK?

Yes, it's fine to use a treadmill. There's nothing quite like walking outside on a fine, sunny day but sometimes life just isn't like that! On dark, cold evenings a treadmill – if you have access to one – can be a useful way to get your walk in. Treadmills offer a more forgiving surface than hard pavement, so can be a little easier on your joints: something to bear in mind if you are returning to walking following an injury. You can follow your usual programme if you are using a treadmill but if you intend doing a 'flat' walk, set the incline at around 1.5 per cent as this is equivalent to walking outside.

CHAPTER 5
WALKING PROGRAMMES

These programmes have been designed as a guide to help you get started. They are not set in stone so if you need to change the sessions around to suit you, go ahead. However, try to complete one week of sessions before you move on to the next week, as the programmes are progressive. This means that they start at a very easy level and gradually become more challenging as the weeks go by. This steady progression will allow your body to recover between exercise sessions, which is important because it's during recovery, rather than exercise itself, that your body makes the adaptations that increase your fitness. Similarly, if you need more time at a certain level, go back a few weeks and work from there.

Have a look at each programme and decide which one you feel suits you best in terms of your current fitness, any medical considerations, how much time you have to exercise and what your goals are. There are checklists with each programme to help you decide.

A word about weight loss

You don't need to do a specific programme for weight loss. What you do need to do is monitor what you are eating and keep on the move. All of these programmes encourage you to do just that. The Beginner programme is particularly suitable because it aims to get you walking 10,000 steps each day, with up to 4,000 of those steps in one session and at a brisk pace. Taking part in other activities in addition to your walking will also help (see page 63).

The programmes are merely a guide, so if you prefer you can write your own, to fit around your other commitments. Whether you are going to follow your own programme or one of the programmes in this book, bear the following exercise principles in mind.

Exercise principles

Exercise programme principles:

F	Frequency
I	Intensity
T	Time
T	Type

Frequency

In other words, how often you exercise. A beginner with low fitness levels would benefit from shorter, more frequent walks. A very fit individual with little time, could walk less frequently but at a higher intensity because their fitness allows them to do so.

Measuring intensity

Knowing the intensity of your exercise session is important to ensure that you are not working unnecessarily hard, but working hard enough to stimulate the cardiovascular system. There are several methods that you can use, and you can use them in combination:

• Talk test

• Borg rate of perceived exertion

• Heart rate

The programmes in this book are based on the rate of perceived exertion scale (RPE) and heart rate, but if you do not want to use a heart rate monitor and find the RPE scale difficult to get used to, you can just use a simple talk test.

The talk test

Able to talk freely or sing throughout the walk
You probably need to increase the pace as you need to get a
little out of breath to challenge your cardiovascular system.

Only able to utter single words between breaths
You are likely to be working anaerobically i.e. you aren't
getting enough oxygen into your system. This is likely to feel
uncomfortable and you should probably slow down or rest
until you are able to speak again.

Able to string a few words together between breaths
You are working aerobically, i.e. you are taking in enough
oxygen to fulfil the needs of your muscles. Just the
right level of intensity.

Rate of perceived exertion (RPE) scale
Devised some 30 years ago by Gunnar Borg, a professor in psychology, this scale
has proved an effective way of quantifying exercise intensity. It is a subjective method
based on perceived effort, but it can be used to estimate your heart rate during
exercise. The correlation becomes less accurate with age but can be useful to give a
rough idea in the absence of a heart rate monitor. Simply take the perceived exertion
rating and multiply by 10 to give you an estimated heart rate. So a perceived exertion
of 15 (hard) would result in a heart rate of around 150 beats per minute.

Borg's rate of perceived exertion scale

6	*No exertion at all*
7	*Extremely light*
8	
9	*Very light*
10	
11	*Light*
12	
13	*Somewhat hard*
14	
15	*Hard*
16	
17	*Very hard*
18	
19	*Extremely hard*
20	*Maximal exertion*

Most of the sessions in the beginner and intermediate programmes will be between
RPE 10–15, as this will bring about good fitness gains initially. The more advanced
programmes will also include interval sessions and walks that are classed as 'very
hard' which are needed to keep stimulating improvement.

Heart rate
Heart rate increases with intensity during exercise so it is a reliable indicator of how

hard you are working. To get fitter, you need to keep your heart rate in your 'target zone' for a suitable duration. The target heart rate will vary depending on your age, fitness level and resting heart rate.

Working out target heart rate using the Karvonen Formula

You will need to know:
1 Your age-predicted maximum heart rate (MHR):
   men = 220 minus age
   women = 226 minus age

2 Your resting heart rate (see page 8)

3 The percentage intensity that you want to work at. For most people an intensity of between 50 and 80 per cent of maximum heart rate is a good range to work within and is an efficient way to increase cardiovascular fitness. If you are unfit, you should start at the lower intensities to begin with. People who are very fit can train at intensities higher than 80 per cent, but this is not necessary for most types of walking training.

Example
Below is the formula that you need to use to work out percentages of MHR. I've given an example to show how it works. Robert, a 31-year-old male, has a resting heart rate of 65 beats per minute. He wants to work out what 70 per cent of his maximum heart rate is:

Age-predicted max. heart rate 220 - 31= 189

Subtract resting heart rate	- 65
Gives you the heart rate reserve	= 124
Multiply this by required percentage	70% (0.7)
Which gives you	87
Add the resting heart rate back in	+65

Which gives you   = 152

So, if Robert works at 70 per cent of his MHR his heart rate will be 152 bpm.

*The age-predicted maximum heart rate is just a guide. Your
true MHR may be ten beats higher or lower. To find out your
true MHR you would need to undertake a maximal test. This
is a 'stepped' test with intensity increasing every few minutes
or so until the MHR is achieved. By its very nature this test is
stressful on the body and should only be undertaken by
those who are already quite fit and well with no medical
issues or past history of heart problems. You should take
advice from your doctor and only undertake a test like this
with a fully-qualified fitness professional or an exercise
physiologist. If you are unfit you may not be able to reach
your true MHR as you will want to stop the test before you
reach it! It is also worth remembering that it is highly unlikely
that you will reach your maximum heart rate while walking
unless on a very steep gradient at speed.*

Warming up

A basic warm-up need only take a few minutes and is a great way to prepare
both the body and mind for your walking session. A walk of about 5 minutes,
followed by some mobilizing exercises is all that is required.

Did you know?
*Recent research suggests that stretching prior to exercise is
not as important as was once thought and that steadily
increasing body temperature is more important to prevent
injury. However, stretching after your walk when your muscles
are warm is both important and enjoyable.*

Effects of warming-up on the body
- A good warm-up raises body temperature, increases blood flow and therefore
  supplies more oxygen to the muscles that need it.

- Muscles become more 'elastic' as body temperature increases. This makes them
  less prone to injury. Imagine the difference between stretching a cold piece of Blu
  Tack® and a warm piece – the cold piece will tear readily, whereas the warmer
  piece has some 'give' in it. It is just the same with our muscles.

- Muscles become more efficient as they warm up so everything feels easier.

- Lubrication to your joints increases gradually during the warm-up, improving their mobility and making them less susceptible to injury.

Effect of warming-up on the mind

- Warming-up will increase your motivation. If you are suffering from a lack of enthusiasm tell yourself you will just do the warm-up. Nine times out of ten you will find yourself completing a whole walk! This is because the body starts to produce endorphins or 'feelgood' hormones even during gentle exercise.

Warm-up routine

Start walking slowly for a couple of minutes before gradually increasing the pace. Use this time to focus on good posture and walking technique. By the end of 5 minutes you should be walking briskly. If you are not actually feeling warm at this stage add another 2 or 3 minutes, particularly during the cooler winter months. Now complete some mobility exercises (listed below) while you are walking to help lubricate the joints. About 30 seconds of each will suffice.

- High knee walking – exaggerate the knee lift as you walk.

- 'Butt' kicking – your own that is, not someone else's! Concentrate on bringing your heel up to your bottom as you walk, but take care not to overdo it.

- Exaggerated arms – swing your arms back and forth a few times and then follow these with some big circles – both forwards and backwards – to really get your upper body moving.

- Hip tapping – as you walk tap the hip of your lead leg with your opposite hand. This introduces a gentle swing from the waist and shoulders which helps to activate core muscles and releases tension in the upper body.

Now you're ready to go. If you have any particularly tight muscles, only stretch them gently at this point. The calf and Achilles tendon stretch on page 54 is a good one to do before you set off as these muscles can become a little tight in walkers.

Cooling down

Just as it is important to gradually warm-up the body, it is equally important to cool it down gradually, ending the exercise session with some well-chosen stretches.

If you stop exercising abruptly there can be a tendency for blood to 'pool' in the extremities, especially in the legs. This can make you feel nauseous and a little dizzy, so slowing down towards the end of your walk, particularly if it has been a long or fast walk, will help to avoid this. It may also help to reduce any muscle soreness which can occur the following day. The cool-down also allows you time to consider the feeling of satisfaction and well-being that exercise can bring.

Cool-down routine

- After you finish your walk, or before you reach home, slow down your pace and continue to walk for a few more minutes.

- Find somewhere suitable to stretch. In summer, you can stretch outside, but in the winter you will need to stretch inside in the warm, preferably on a mat.

- Work through the stretches on the following pages, making sure that you take your time for each one. Go into each stretch gently, hold for at least 15–20 seconds and try not to bounce. Never stretch a muscle to the point where it becomes painful.

- Remember to breathe while holding a stretch.

- Start with your standing stretches and gradually work down, so that you finish with a full-body stretch, lying on the floor.

Stretching tip

When you come back from a walk, especially a long or fast one, you need to remember that the muscles in the lower body may be quite tired. Tired muscles are already stressed muscles. When you stretch a muscle you are adding to that stress a little more, so stretching gently is key. What you want to achieve by doing these stretches is to take the muscles back to their pre-walk length. If you want to work on increasing your flexibility you would be well-advised to take a 10-minute walk to warm up and then do a specific stretching session for its own sake, holding each stretch for at least 30 seconds.

Standing stretches

Calf stretch

1 Stand facing a wall with your feet hip-width apart. Place both hands on the wall a little more than shoulder-width apart.

2 Take a step backwards with both legs until you feel a gentle stretch in your calf muscles. Pull your tummy button in towards your spine while in this position to support your back and try to keep your heels on the ground – if you can't keep your heels down step a little closer to the wall until you can.

3 Hold the stretch for 15–20 seconds.

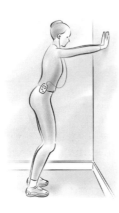

Achilles stretch

1 Once you have stretched your calf muscles, take a small step closer to the wall keeping your feet hip-width apart.

2 Bend both knees, keeping your heels on the ground. You should feel a stretch in the lower half of your calf muscles, going down into your ankles.

3 Hold this stretch for 15–20 seconds.

Hamstring stretch

1 From a standing position, step forwards with your right foot. Place your heel on the ground and pull your toes gently towards you, keeping your leg straight but not locked at the knee.

2 Now lean forward from the hips, keeping your spine in a neutral position, until you can feel a gentle stretch in your hamstring muscles at the back of your thighs.

3 You can place both hands at the top of your left thigh for support. Don't put them on the same leg you are stretching as pushing down can encourage you to lock out your knee.

4 Hold for 20–30 seconds and repeat on the other leg.

Upper back stretch
1 Stand tall with your feet hip-width apart.

2 Take both arms above your head* and hold your right wrist with your left hand. Pull yourself over to the left so that you flex from your waist. You should feel a gentle stretch on your right-hand side, going from your waist to your upper arms.

3 Hold for 15–20 seconds and then change sides.

* Note: If you suffer from high blood pressure it is better if you don't raise your arms above your head. As an alternative, place your hands on your hips and then bend to each side, holding the stretch for 15–20 seconds.

Chest stretch
1 Stand tall with your feet hip-width apart.

2 Hold your hands behind your back and gently draw your arms back until you can feel a stretch across the front of your chest and shoulders.

3 Hold this stretch for 15–20 seconds, making sure that you don't arch your lower back.

All-fours

Cat stretch

1 Start from an all-fours position, with your spine in a neutral position (see page 39). Imagine you have a string attached to your back and that it's pulling you upwards. Look down towards the mat.

2 Hold for 5–10 seconds and then gently allow your back to sink down towards the mat. Lift your head and look forwards. Just stretch to a point that is comfortable, don't overarch your back. Hold for 5–10 seconds. Repeat each stretch three times.

Seated

Adductor stretch

1 Start in a seated position, sit tall. Place the soles of your feet together and hold your shins. Gently ease your knees down to the floor until you can feel a stretch on the insides of your thighs.

2 Hold this stretch for 15–20 seconds, making sure you continue to sit tall.

Prone lying

Quad stretch

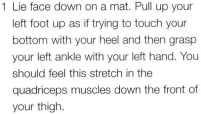

1 Lie face down on a mat. Pull up your left foot up as if trying to touch your bottom with your heel and then grasp your left ankle with your left hand. You should feel this stretch in the quadriceps muscles down the front of your thigh.

2 If you can't feel it, ease your foot closer to your bottom until you can. Think about pressing your hip bones down into the mat a little to increase the stretch at the top of your thighs.

3 Hold this stretch for 15–20 seconds and then repeat on the right leg.

Back lying

Hip stretch

1 Lie on your back with both knees bent and your feet flat on the floor. Take your right foot and place it so that the outside of your ankle rests on your left knee. Your right hip and knee will turn out as you do this.

2 Gently push your right knee away from you so that you feel a stretch in the outside of your right hip. If you can't feel the stretch here, place your hand under your left knee and gently pull it towards you raising your foot off the floor, keeping your right ankle in place. Now you should definitely feel it!

3 Hold for 15–20 seconds if it is comfortable to do so, then repeat, starting with the left leg.

Full body stretch

1 Lie on your back. Straighten your legs, making sure your back doesn't arch, and take your arms behind your head.

Softly point your toes and lengthen your body, thinking in particular about your spine. Think of yourself growing a couple of centimetres on the mat but don't overstretch and don't forget to breathe!

2 Hold the stretch for 15–20 seconds, then relax.

4 Repeat the same stretch but pull your toes towards you and push your heels away so that you emphasize the stretch in the calf muscles and Achilles tendon. Hold for 15–20 seconds and relax.

Your cool-down is complete.

Core strength routine

The following exercises will help to strengthen core muscles involved in maintaining good posture. If you have any back problems you should take advice from a medical professional before doing these exercises. Walk for 5–10 minutes to warm up before you start. All of the exercises should be done on a mat.

Table tops

1 Start in an all-fours position. Draw your tummy button up towards your spine which should be in a neutral position (see page 39). Keeping your hips and shoulders level, stretch one arm out in front of you. At the same time, stretch out your opposite leg, raising it to about hip height.

2 Alternate slowly from one side to the other, breathing out as you stretch, and breathing in to return to the start position. Complete 16 stretches.

Alternatives

If you find balancing a problem, leave both hands on the floor or keep your toes in contact with the floor as you stretch out your leg.

Knee raises

1 Lie on your back with your knees bent and your spine in a neutral position (see page 39). Draw your navel towards your spine to activate your deep core muscles. Lift your right knee towards your chest, then the left.

2 Lower your right leg, followed by the left, keeping them bent at the knee. As you lift and lower your legs don't allow your back to arch and try to keep your hips level. Breathe in before each movement and breathe out during movement.

3 Repeat 12 times slowly. If you want to increase the challenge you can take both legs down together but you must be able to maintain a neutral spine.

String of pearls

Before you start this exercise picture a pearl necklace lying on a table. Imagine holding it at one end and slowing picking it up, so it lifts from the table one pearl at a time. The movement of the necklace would be very fluid. That's what we want to achieve in your spine with this exercise. This is an excellent exercise to include with your stretches post-walk as it really mobilizes the spine. Be gentle though and don't try to make your spine act like a string of pearls if it just won't! Most of us have areas, particularly in our lower backs, which are quite stiff so just slow down through those points.

1 Lie on your back, knees bent, draw your navel towards your spine and let your arms relax by your sides.

2 Take a breath in to prepare and then, as you breathe out, lead with your tail bone and start to roll your spine up from the mat. Let your hips come up and continue rolling up until you are in a slope position. Picture your vertebrae coming up off the mat one by one.

3 Take a breath in to prepare and then, as you breathe out, slowly return to the start position, visualizing your vertebrae touching the mat, one by one, on the way down. Repeat ten times.

Criss-cross

1 Lie on your back with your knees bent and one hand by each ear. Keep your elbows pointing out to the sides rather than straight forward. Draw your navel towards your spine.

2 In a simultaneous movement, lift your left knee and take your right shoulder up and across to the left to meet your knee. Breathe out to come up and over, take a breath in at the top and then breathe out again as you lower to the start position.

3 Alternate from one side to the other and repeat 16 times, 8 on each side.

Swim stretch

1 Lie face down with your arms stretched out in front of you and your legs straight out behind you. Try to lengthen your spine as if someone is pulling a string from the top of your head. Gently pull your navel up to your spine, away from the mat.

2 Breathe out and stretch one arm and the opposite leg until they lift from the mat. Breathe in and lower.

3 Alternate from one side to the other and repeat 16 times, 8 on each side.

Rollbacks

1 Sit tall with your knees bent and your heels on the floor. Draw your navel to your spine, shoulders down and back. Hold on to your thighs very gently for support. Tuck your tail bone underneath you and roll back to a level where you can feel your abdominal muscles starting to work, keeping your heels in contact with the floor. Slowly return to the start position. Repeat six times.

2 Roll back (think of the String of pearls exercise here with your 'rolling') until you reach a point where your feet feel light and you can really feel your abdominals working. Roll up in a controlled manner. Repeat six times.

3 Roll slowly all the way back to the floor, taking your arms out behind you when you get there. Take a breath in and as you breathe out take your arms back over your head and roll back up to the start position.

4 If you find it difficult to roll up, and lots of people do, use your arms to help you a little. (Practise the String of pearls exercise as this will help to mobilize your spine.) Repeat four–six times.

Gym ball push-ups

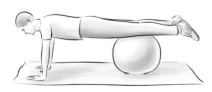

1 Kneel behind the ball and then roll over the top of it, walking forwards with your hands as you do so. The further away you move from the ball the harder this exercise will be, so start with the ball under your hips initially. You can make it more difficult as the weeks progress. Make sure that you support your back in this position by drawing your navel up towards your spine.

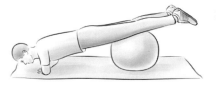

2 Perform 12 push-ups with your hands a little wider than shoulder width, breathing in as you go down to the floor and breathing out to push up from the floor.

Gym ball plank

1 Kneel behind the ball, with your hands resting on top of it. Roll the ball away from you until your body is in a straight line from your shoulders to your hips. Check your posture and make sure that your back is in a neutral position (see page 39) and your elbows are under your shoulders.

2 Pull your navel towards your spine to activate your core muscles. You should feel a tightness around your abdominal muscles, rather like wearing a very wide belt. Hold this position for 10 seconds initially, building up as you get stronger. Repeat five times. Breathe throughout the exercise.

3 If you want to increase the challenge you can either straighten your arms a little by pushing your elbows away or straighten your legs so that you are supported only by your toes and your elbows. This is very challenging and good posture is important. You must ensure that your back remains in a neutral position and keep drawing navel to spine all the time. Don't hold your breath.

Varying your exercise routine

Engaging in other activities from time to time in addition to walking is really important to keep a balance in your exercise routine. It allows tired muscles to recover by using them in a different way and will keep you feeling mentally fresh so that you can go out and achieve whatever goals you have set yourself. Our bodies also need to be challenged in different ways to keep improving. Any exercise that raises your heart rate for 20 minutes or more will be of benefit.

Cycling

Cycling is great for toning the muscles in your legs and is also a good low-impact cardiovascular exercise. If you have a bike tucked away somewhere, look it out and get it serviced at your local cycle shop. Ask them to set it up for you so that you are comfortable and efficient, then go explore! Don't forget to wear a helmet and padded cycling shorts are a must if you are going to be out for longer than 30 minutes as these are much more comfortable. If you don't want to go out cycling, try a spinning class or use a stationary bike if you have access to one.

Swimming

Swimming uses lots of different muscle groups and it can be a great cardiovascular exercise. If you aren't confident in the water, book yourself some lessons to improve your technique. Your instructor will also be able to give you some ideas as to what you can do in your swim sessions.

Rowing

Rowing requires the use of all the major muscle groups and will work your cardiovascular system hard. Good technique is important to get the most out of your rowing sessions. Bad technique could cause more harm than good so ask at your gym if you are unsure. If you live near a rowing club call in and ask about having a go. Many rowing clubs have 'try rowing' days where beginners can join in and go out on the water and there is usually a good club atmosphere. But beware, rowing is very addictive!

Other ideas

• Dancing

• Fitness classes – there are so many, from Pilates to circuit training to aquaerobics. Call in at your local leisure centre and see what's on offer, or search the Internet for activities in your area.

• Badminton, tennis or squash – if you don't know how to play, ask about coaching.

Beginner programme

See keywords on page 66.

Week	Mon	Tues	Wed	Thurs
1 Average steps + 500 daily	Timed walk: 1000 steps Stretches	Rest	1500 steps RPE 10–11 Stretches	Rest
2 Average steps + 700 daily	1000 steps RPE 10–11 Stretches	Rest	1500 steps RPE 10–11 Stretches	1500 steps RPE 10–11 Stretches
3 Average steps + 900 daily	2000 steps RPE 12–13 Stretches	2000 steps RPE 10–11 Stretches	Rest Core strength	2000 steps RPE 12–13 Stretches
4 Average steps + 1000 daily	2500 steps RPE 12–13 Stretches	Rest Core strength	2500 steps RPE 12–13 Stretches	2500 steps RPE 10–11 Stretches
5 Average steps + 1100 daily	3000 steps RPE 12–13 Stretches	Rest	2500 steps RPE 12–13 Core strength Stretches	2500 steps RPE 12–13 Stretches
6 Average steps + 1100 daily	2000 steps RPE 12–13 Stretches	2000 steps RPE 10–11 Core strength Stretches	Rest	3000 steps RPE 12–13 Stretches

Fri	Sat	Sun	Total Steps
1500 steps RPE 10–11 Stretches	Rest	2000 steps RPE 10–11 Stretches	6000 Timed walk:
2000 steps RPE 10–11 Stretches	Rest	2000 steps RPE 10–11 Stretches	8000
2000 steps RPE 10–11 Stretches	Rest	2000 steps RPE 12–13 Stretches	10000
2000 steps, split 1000 RPE 12–13 1000 RPE 14–15 Stretches	Rest	2500 steps RPE 12–13 Core strength Stretches	12000
3000 steps RPE 10–11 Stretches	Core strength	3000 steps, split 1500 RPE 12–13 1500 RPE 14–15 Stretches	14000
2000 steps RPE 10–11 Core strength Stretches	Rest	Timed walk: 1000 steps Stretches	10000 Timed walk:

Week	Mon	Tues	Wed	Thurs
7 Average steps + 1200 daily	2500 steps RPE 12–13 Stretches	Rest Core strength	2500 steps RPE 12–13 Stretches	2500 steps RPE 12–13 Stretches
8 Average steps + 1300 daily	3000 steps RPE 12–13 Stretches	Rest	2500 steps RPE 14–15 Stretches	2500 steps RPE 12–13 Stretches
9 Average steps + 1400 daily	3000 steps RPE 14–15 Stretches	Rest	3000 steps RPE 12–13 Stretches	3500 steps RPE 12–13 Stretches
10 Average steps + 1500 daily	3500 steps RPE 14–15 Stretches	Rest	3500 steps RPE 12–13 Core strength Stretches	3500 steps RPE 14–15 Stretches

KEYWORDS

Average steps + XX — As well as following the programme, for the next week you should try to walk the given number of extra steps in addition to your usual daily total. See below for further information.

RPE — Rate of perceived exertion (see page 49).

Timed walk — Find a route which is approximately 1,000 steps or 800 metres and walk it as fast as you comfortably can. Time it and record the time in the Total steps box.

Fri	Sat	Sun	Total Steps
2000 steps, split 1000 RPE 12–13 1000 RPE 14–15 Stretches	Rest	2500 steps RPE 10–11 Core strength Stretches	12000
3000 steps RPE 14–15 Stretches	Core strength	3000 steps, split 1500 RPE 12–13 1500 RPE 14–15 Stretches	14000
3000 steps RPE 14–15 Stretches	Core strength	3500 steps, split 2000 RPE 12–13 1500 RPE 14–15 Stretches	16000
2500 steps RPE 12–13 Stretches	Timed walk: 1000 steps Stretches	4000 steps, split 2000 RPE 12–13 2000 RPE 14–15 Stretches	18000 Timed Walk

Core strength   Four exercises – Table tops, Knee raises, String of pearls, Criss-cross (see pages 58–59).

Stretches   See pages 54–57.

Beginner programme

The aim of the programme

This programme introduces you to a routine that's manageable, enjoyable and effective – all factors that will make your programme easier to stick to. It also aims to get you up to the magic 10,000 steps each day. As well as keeping a walking diary try recording your weekly step totals in a chart so that you can easily see your progress.

Is this programme right for me?

- Did it take you longer than 20 minutes to do your 1-mile walk test (see page 18)?

- Are you overweight?

- Are you sedentary (inactive)?

- Has it been a long time since you last exercised (i.e. months or years)?
If you answered 'yes' to most of the above questions then this programme should be suitable for you .

Note: If you answered 'yes' to any of the questions in the Health and fitness safety-first box on page 15, you should seek advice from your doctor before you start this exercise programme.

Who could benefit from this programme?

- those suffering from depression/anxiety.

- people with osteoporosis*.

- pregnant women* (see page 100–2).

- the core strength element of this programme coupled with improvements in posture make it beneficial for people with back pain*.

- diabetics*.

- asthmatics* (see page 103).

- those recovering from cardiac illness*.

* NOTE: You should check with your doctor before starting this exercise programme.

About the programme

Using a pedometer

This programme requires a pedometer, which is inexpensive and useful to keep track of your steps and/or distance (see page 33). On average it takes people around 1,200 steps to cover a 1 kilometre. Bear in mind though that this is an average and that stride length does vary. The actual number of steps in a mile could be anywhere between 1,100 and 1,500. In setting up your pedometer you will find out what your stride length is. If you work roughly to 1,200 steps to a kilometre you can easily work out how long your walk will take and what would be a suitable route.

What if I don't want to use a pedometer?

No problem. Calculate your stride length. If the walk session is, for example, 2,000 steps, just multiply this by your stride length to ascertain the distance. Then you can find a route that is approximately this distance.

What does 'average steps' mean?

On the left-hand side of the programme you will see 'average steps + xx daily'. Before you start your programme, wear a pedometer every day for five days and write down how many steps you do each day. Add up the daily totals and divide by five to give you your average number of daily steps. If this is above 6,000 steps per day you could consider following the Intermediate programme. The '+' figure is the number of extra steps that you should try to take every day in addition to your average steps and your specific walking sessions. See page 110-111 for ways to fit more walking into your everyday life.

Why can't I add extra steps to the specified walking sessions?

To increase cardiovascular fitness, exercise needs to be sustained at the right intensity for a suitable duration, ideally 20 minutes or more. As a beginner the sessions in the programme will provide enough intensity for you. It wouldn't be a good idea for you to try and walk your 10,000 steps at that same intensity just yet as you could end up injuring yourself, particularly if you are not used to walking.

The sessions

- Important: make sure you warm up and cool down for each session (see pages 52–59).

- The sessions are initially quite short in duration as it is more important at this stage to get used to the routine of exercising. The walks gradually increase in both duration and intensity as the weeks progress. As the pace quickens, make sure that you are thinking about technique and posture and if you find this difficult, drop the pace a little.

- The total steps increase each week, up to week 6 which is a recovery week. Use this week to recharge your batteries, physically and mentally, and reflect on the good work you have done. Read over your training diary – you may already notice that you are covering a certain route a little quicker or finding it easier. There are three timed walks in the programme to help you monitor your progress. Make sure you record these times on the programme itself or in your training diary. If you have found the programme difficult up to this point you could go back and repeat weeks 1–6 before carrying on with the remaining weeks.

Rest days
- You still have your 'extra' steps to fit into the day, but no structured walking session. If you are feeling energetic and keen, try doing another activity such as swimming or cycling or try something new like a yoga or Pilates class. But feel free to take the day off without feeling guilty and plan your next walk.

If you complete this programme...
You will be a fitter, happier person! After you have finished the programme it is a good idea to have a week off from a structured routine. Try different activities and think about what you would like to do next. You could look into entering a charity walk for example (see page 112) and perhaps follow the 5 weeks to 5 km programme on page 86. If you want to develop your fitness further why not try the Intermediate programme?

Intermediate programme

KEYWORDS

RPE

Rate of perceived exertion (see page 50).

*

If you need a change from walking you can do another activity in these sessions. Try swimming or cycling for example. Keep duration and intensity similar.

Core strength

Six exercises – Table tops, Knee raises, String of pearls, Criss-cross, Swim stretch and Rollbacks (see pages 58–61).

Intervals

Short bursts of fast walking to inject pace. Allow at least an equal number of steps recovery between each interval.

Timed walk

Find a route which is approximately 2,000 steps or 1.5 kilometres and walk it as fast as you comfortably can. Time it and record the time in the Total steps box.

Stretches

See page 54. Stretching after your walks is important, so if you are tight on time cut the walk short by a few minutes if you need to rather than missing them out.

Intermediate programme

Week	Mon	Tues	Wed	Thurs
1	4000 steps RPE 12–13 Stretches	Core strength Stretches	Timed walk: 2000 steps Stretches	4000 steps RPE 12–13 Stretches
2	4000 steps RPE 12–13 Stretches	Core strength Stretches	5000 steps RPE 12–13 Stretches	3500 steps* RPE 14–15 Stretches
3	4000 steps RPE 14–15 Stretches	Core strength Stretches	6000 steps RPE 12–13 Stretches	4000 steps RPE 14–15 Stretches
4	5000 steps RPE 12–13 Stretches	Core strength Stretches	6000 steps RPE 12–13 Stretches	5000 steps RPE 14–15 Stretches
5	5000 steps RPE 12–13 Stretches	Core strength Stretches	6000 steps RPE 14–15 Stretches	5000 steps RPE 12–13 Stretches
6	5000 steps RPE 14–15 Stretches	Core strength Stretches	6000 steps RPE 12–13 Stretches	4000 steps* RPE 14–15 Stretches

Fri	Sat	Sun	Total Steps
Core strength Stretches	Rest	4000 steps RPE 14–15 Stretches	14000 Timed walk:
Core strength Stretches	Rest	5000 steps RPE 14–15 Stretches	17000
Core strength Stretches	Rest	6000 steps RPE 14–15 Stretches	20000
Core strength Stretches	Rest	7000 steps RPE 14–15 Stretches	23000
Core strength Stretches	Rest	10000 steps RPE 10–11 Stretches	26000
Core strength Stretches	4000 steps RPE 12–13 Stretches	Timed walk: 2000 steps Stretches	20000 Timed walk:

Week	Mon	Tues	Wed	Thurs
7	5000 steps RPE 14–15 Stretches	Core strength Stretches	6000 steps – increase pace every 1500 steps from RPE 10–11, 12–13, 14–15, max. pace Stretches	5000 steps RPE 14–15 Stretches
8	6000 steps RPE 14–15 Stretches	Core strength Stretches	Intervals 8000 steps RPE 12–13 including 5 x 200 steps as fast as comfortably possible Stretches	6000 steps* RPE 14–15 Stretches
9	Intervals 8000 steps RPE 12–13 including 6 x 200 steps as fast as comfortably possible Stretches	Core strength Stretches	8000 steps – increase pace every 2000 steps from RPE 10–11, 12–13, 14–15, max. pace Stretches	6000 steps RPE 14–15 Stretches
10	Intervals 8000 steps RPE 12–13 including 4 x 300 steps as fast as comfortably possible Stretches	Core strength Stretches	10000 steps RPE 14–15 Stretches	4000 steps* RPE 12–13 Stretches

Fri	Sat	Sun	Total Steps
Core strength Stretches	Rest	Intervals 8000 steps RPE 12–13 including 4 x 200 steps as fast as comfortably possible Stretches	24000
Core strength Stretches	Rest	10000 steps RPE 12–13 Stretches	28000
Core strength Stretches	Rest	12000 steps RPE 12–13 Stretches	32000
Timed walk: 2000 steps Stretches	Rest	14000 steps RPE 12–13 Stretches	36000 Timed walk

The aim of the programme

The aim of this programme is to enable you to walk all of the recommended 10,000 daily steps (approximately 8 kilometres) in one go. The longest walk is 14,000 steps (approximately 12 kilometres) so when you have completed it you will be more than ready to move on to the Advanced programme (see page 80) if you want to.

Is this programme right for me?

• Did you complete the 1-mile walk test (see page 18) in 18–20 minutes?

• Have you already completed the Beginners programme (see page 66)?

• Would you consider yourself relatively active?

If you answered 'yes' to the above questions, then this programme should be suitable for you.

Note: If you answered 'yes' to any of the questions in the Health and fitness safety-first box on page 15, you should seek advice from your doctor before you start this exercise programme.

About the programme

Using a pedometer

This programme is based on using a pedometer. If you don't have a pedometer see page 33 to help you calculate the distance for each walk (1,200 steps is approximately 1 kilometre).

The sessions
- Important: make sure you warm up and cool down for each session (see pages 52–59).

- There are three timed walks in the programme to help you monitor your progress. Make sure you record these times on the programme itself or in your training diary.

- The first 6 weeks of this programme will help to develop your muscular and cardiovascular endurance. The length of the walks gradually increases, along with the intensity, but if you need more time you can repeat each week before moving on to the next one. Make the programme work for you and remember that consistency is the key.

- The second half of the programme continues to work on endurance and introduces interval training to develop pace. Interval training uses a series of relatively short 'bursts' of higher intensity walking to boost the heart rate. As the pace increases think about maintaining good technique and posture.

Advanced/half marathon programme

See keywords on page 82.

Week	Mon	Tues	Wed	Thurs
1	Timed walk: 3 km Stretches	5 km 55–65% MHR Stretches	Rest*	5 km 55–65% MHR Stretches
2	5 km 65–75% MHR Stretches	6 km 55–65% MHR Stretches	Core strength Stretches	Rest
3	Core strength Stretches	6 km 55–65% MHR Stretches	10 km 55–65% MHR Stretches	Rest
4	8 km 55–65% MHR Stretches	Rest	6 km 65–75% MHR Stretches	Core strength Stretches
5	6 km 65–75% MHR Stretches	Core strength Stretches	8 km 55–65% MHR Stretches	Rest*
6	6 km 65–75% MHR Stretches	6 km 65–75% MHR Stretches	Rest*	6 km 65–75% MHR Stretches
7	6 km 65–75% MHR Stretches	Intervals 6 km 55–65% MHR with 3 mins out of 15 walked at 75–85% MHR Stretches	Core strength Stretches	Rest

Fri	Sat	Sun	Total km
Core strength Stretches	Rest	6 km 55–65% MHR Stretches	19 Timed walk:
5 km 65–75% MHR Stretches	6 km 55–65% MHR Stretches	Rest*	22
5 km 65–75% MHR Stretches	Core strength Stretches	5 km 65–75% MHR Stretches	26
5 km 65–75% MHR Stretches	Rest*	10 km 55–65% MHR Stretches	29
6 km 65–75% MHR Stretches	11 km 65–75% MHR Stretches	Core strength Stretches	31
Core strength Stretches	Rest	Timed walk: 3 km	21 Timed walk
6 km 65–75% MHR Stretches	Intervals 6 km 65–75% MHR with 3 mins out of 15 walked at 75–85% MHR Stretches	Rest*	24

Week	Mon	Tues	Wed	Thurs
8	Core strength Stretches	Intervals 6 km 55–65% MHR with 4 mins out of 15 walked at 75–85% MHR Stretches	8 km 65–75% MHR Stretches	Rest
9	Rest*	Intervals 6 km 55–65% MHR with 5 mins out of 15 walked at 75–85% MHR Stretches	10 km 65–75% MHR Stretches	Core strength Stretches
10	Intervals 8 km 55–65% MHR with 5 mins out of 15 walked at 75–85% MHR Stretches	Core strength Stretches	6 km 65–75% MHR Stretches	Rest
11	Intervals 8 km 55–65% MHR with 5 mins out of 15 walked at 75–85% MHR Stretches	Core strength Stretches	8 km 65–75 % MHR Stretches	Rest*

Fri	Sat	Sun	Total Miles
Intervals 6 km 65–75% MHR with 4 mins out of 15 walked at 75–85% MHR Stretches	Core strength Stretches	8 km 65–75% MHR Stretches	28
Intervals 6 km 65–75% MHR with 5 mins out of 15 walked at 75–85% MHR Stretches	10 km 65–75% MHR Stretches	Rest	32
Intervals 8 km 65–75% MHR with 5 mins out of 15 walked at 75–85% MHR Stretches	6 km 65–75% MHR Stretches	Core strength Stretches	28
Intervals 6 km 65–75% MHR with 5 mins out of 15 walked at 75–85% MHR Stretches	10 km 65–75% MHR Stretches	Timed walk: 3 km Stretches	35 Timed walk:

Week	Mon	Tues	Wed	Thurs
12	Rest*	Intervals 8 km 55–65% MHR with 6 mins out of 15 walked at 75–85% MHR Stretches	8 km 65–75 % MHR Stretches	Core strength Stretches
13	Intervals 6 km 55–65% MHR with 7 mins out of 15 walked at 75–85% MHR Stretches	Core strength Stretches	10 km 65–75% MHR Stretches	Rest
14	Rest	Intervals 6 km 55-65% MHR with 6 mins out of 15 walked at 75-85% MHR Stretches	5 km 65–75% MHR Stretches	Core strength Stretches
15	Intervals 3 miles 55–65% MHR with 5 mins out of 15 walked at 75–85% MHR Stretches	Core strength Stretches	3 km 65–75% MHR Stretches	3 km 65–75% MHR Stretches

KEYWORDS

Rest* Either take a rest day or enjoy another activity of your choice. 'A change is as good as a rest' don't forget!

Core strength The exercises on pages 60–61.

Intervals Short bursts of fast walking to inject pace. Try to space them evenly through your walk.

Fri	Sat	Sun	Total Miles
Intervals 6 km 65–75% MHR with 6 mins out of 15 walked at 75–85% MHR Stretches	13 km 65–75% MHR Stretches	Rest	36
Intervals 6 km 65–75% MHR with 7 mins out of 15 walked at 75–85% MHR Stretches	Core strength Stretches	10 miles 65–75% MHR Stretches	38
Intervals 6 km 65–75% MHR with 6 mins out of 15 walked at 75–85% MHR Stretches	5 km 65–75% MHR Stretches	Rest*	22
Rest	Rest	Half marathon Good luck!	11

Timed walk	Find a route which is approximately 3 kilometres and walk it as fast as you comfortably can. Time it and record the time in the Total kilometres box.
Stretches	Stretching after your walks is important so if you are tight on time cut the walk short by a few minutes if you need to rather than missing them out.

The aim of the programme

The aim of this programme is to give you the confidence and the endurance to walk a half marathon which is 21 kilometres.

Is this programme right for me?

• Can you complete the 1-mile walk test (see page 18) in 15–18 minutes?

• Have you already completed the Intermediate programme (see page 73) comfortably?

• Would you consider yourself active?

If you answered 'yes' to any two of the questions above then this programme should be suitable for you.

Note: If you answered 'yes' to any of the questions in the Health and fitness safety-first box on page 15, you should seek advice from your doctor before you start this exercise programme. Some of the walks in this programme are of more than 2 hours duration.

About the programme

The first 6 weeks of this programme will develop your endurance.

The second half of the programme continues to work on endurance and introduces interval training to develop pace. Interval training uses a series of relatively short 'bursts' of higher intensity walking to boost the heart rate. As the pace increases think about maintaining good technique and posture.

Heart rate

Look back at page 57 and calculate your heart rates for the different percentage MHR intensities. Write the heart rates on your programme so that you can refer to them easily. This programme is based around the use of a heart rate monitor. If you don't have one, don't worry, you can still complete the programme. Either measure your heart rate by taking your pulse for 10 seconds and multiplying it by 6 to give you the beats per minute, or use the following as a guide:

55–65% HRM	moderate walking pace
65–75% HRM	brisk walking pace
75–85% HRM	fast walking pace

Remember this is just a guide. Some people will find they can easily reach their target heart rate while walking relatively slowly, whereas others will have to walk fairly fast just to achieve the 55–65% HRM level.

The sessions

• Important: make sure you warm up and cool down for each session (see pages 52–59).

5 weeks to 5km programme

See keywords on page 82.

Week	Mon	Tues	Wed	Thurs
1	Time trial: 30 mins as fast as you comfortably can – note distance Stretches	Rest	30 mins RPE 12–13 Stretches	Rest*
2	40 mins RPE 12–13 Stretches	Rest	40 mins RPE 12–13 Stretches	Rest*
3	50 mins RPE 12–13	Rest	Intervals 40 mins RPE 12–13 including 2 mins max. pace every 10 mins Stretches	Rest*
4	Time trial: 30 mins as fast as you comfortably can – note distance Stretches	Rest	Intervals 40 mins RPE 12–13 including 3 mins max. pace every 10 mins Stretches	Rest*
5	40 mins RPE 12–13 Stretches	Rest	Intervals 40 mins RPE 12–13 including 2 mins max. pace every 10 mins Stretches	Rest*

Fri	Sat	Sun	Total Time
30 mins RPE 14–15 Stretches	Rest	30 mins RPE 12–13 Stretches	2 hrs Time trial distance:
30 mins RPE 14–15 Stretches	Rest	40 mins RPE 12–13 Stretches	2 ½ hrs
50 mins RPE 12–13 Stretches	Rest	40 mins RPE 14–15 Stretches	3 hrs
40 mins RPE 12–13 including 1 mins max. pace every 10 mins Stretches	Rest	50 mins RPE 12–13 Stretches	3 ½ hrs Time trial distance:
40 mins RPE 12–13 Stretches	Rest	5-km event	2 hrs

KEYWORDS

Rest*   Either take a rest day or enjoy another activity of your choice.

Intervals   Short bursts of fast walking to inject pace. Try to space them
                 evenly through your walk.

Time trial   Walk for 30 minutes as fast as you comfortably can and note
                 the distance. This doesn't have to be exact distance, it could
                 be 'as far as the big oak tree on the right', as long as you
                 know what it means for next time!

Stretches   Even if you are tight on time, stretching after walks is
                 important, so cut the walk short by a few minutes if you need
                 to rather than missing them out.

The aim of the programme

This programme is aimed at relatively fit and healthy individuals who would like to
prepare for a 5-kilometre event but who don't have a lot of time train.

Is this programme right for me?

• Are you short of time to exercise but relatively fit?

• Can you complete the 1-mile walk test in 18–20 minutes (see page 18)?

• Have you already completed the Beginner programme comfortably (see page 64)?

• Would you consider yourself active?

If you answered 'yes' to any two of the above questions then this programme is
suitable for you.

Note: If you answered 'yes' to any of the questions in the Health and fitness safety-
first box on page 15, you should seek advice from your doctor before you start this
exercise programme. Some of the walks in this programme require you to walk at
your maximum pace for short periods.

About the programme

This programme is based on perceived exertion (see page 49) and, as with the other programmes, is intended as a guide only. If you want to increase the pace or likewise if you feel you need to slow it down, go ahead.

The 40-minute interval walking sessions are a good way to approach a 5-kilometre event if you are not able to maintain a fast pace all the way around. This gives you the chance to practice.

The programme is a short introduction to walking – you may want to follow on with the Intermediate or Advanced/half marathon programme afterwards and try a longer event.

Use the timed trials to see if you can cover more distance in the 30 minutes as the weeks progress. Even after 3 weeks of walking you should start to notice improvements.

Weight loss is not a specific aim of the programme but, as with the other walking schedules, you may find you lose a few pounds as a desirable side effect!

CHAPTER 6
HEALTH AND SAFETY MATTERS

Walking is one of the safest forms of exercise but it is not completely risk-free and you may encounter the occasional problem. The important thing if you do get a niggle is that you don't try and work through it. This will only prolong the condition and could make it worse so that you end up out of action for much longer. NOTE: The advice given here is general, you should consult a doctor if you develop any symptoms that are a cause for concern.

Feet first

A pair of feet are home to about 250,000 sweat glands which can produce around 300 millilitres of sweat every day. So if you add some friction and heat them up a bit by going for a brisk walk is it any wonder that they complain a little from time to time?

Blisters
Prevention is the key here. Caused by friction, heat and sweating, blisters can be very painful once they have formed so avoiding them in the first place is a priority.

Blister prevention
• Make sure your shoes are a good fit, not too tight and not too loose (see page 26).

• Avoid wearing cotton socks and opt for socks made from technical fibres that will wick moisture away from your skin. You can apply a dusting of talcum powder to the inside of your socks to help keep your feet dry. Take spare socks with you on longer walks and avoid wearing new ones that you have not tried before.

• Lubricating your feet with petroleum jelly can be quite effective as a barrier but not everyone likes the feel of it on their skin. Other barrier products you can try are blister pads which are filled with hydrogel.

Dealing with blisters
So you did everything above and you still got a blister! What now?

- Hopefully your bum bag will contain some blister dressings, so if a blister develops while you are out walking you can cover it quickly. Products like blister pads are good but need to be held in place with adhesive tape so you need to make sure you have this to hand as well.

- When you get back, inspect the damage. If the blister is small, cover it with a plaster. Protect larger blisters with a gauze pad or dressing that you can tape in place. Try to avoid further friction. If the blister is in a position that is causing you discomfort, cover it with a soft dressing pad to protect it. Do not burst the blister yourself.

- If a blister bursts, don't peel off the dead skin. Gently press the area to drain the fluid inside then cover the blister with a sterile dressing.

- Change plasters and dressings regularly.

- Monitor it to check for signs of infection, such as prolonged or worsening soreness, pus or any red tracks coming from the blister itself. Consult your doctor if any of these symptoms develop.

Plantar fasciitis

This is inflammation of the plantar fascia – a band of very tough tissue, running from the heel to the toe – which supports the arch in your foot. The inflammation causes pain and sometimes swelling of the heels, making walking and standing very painful. Pain is often worse in the morning.

There are several reasons why plantar fasciitis may develop:

- Poor walking technique.

- Tightness in the calf, Achilles tendon or foot.

- Overpronation, low or high arches or flat feet.

- Poorly fitting shoes or wearing heels all day and then changing to flat shoes. Also worn-out shoes that allow the foot to overpronate.

- Sudden increase in activity levels.

- Sudden weight gain.

Treatment

As with most conditions, the quicker you deal with plantar fasciitis the better. If you leave this untreated you could be struggling with it upwards of 6 months. Initially, rest is one of the best solutions (see box below). Check your shoes (see page 26). If the insides look worn you should replace them, making sure that new ones have good arch support that will reduce the stress on the plantar fasciia. To reduce inflammation and pain, apply an ice pack to the area and rest with your feet up (see R.I.C.E below). Once it has settled down you would benefit from some gentle stretching of the foot, calf and Achilles tendon areas (see page 59). If it does not settle down, seek medical advice either from your doctor or from a chiropodist.

RICE

Rest the injury. Avoid the activity that caused it.

Ice – apply an ice pack or cold compress for 5–10 minutes at a time. This will decrease blood flow to the area and reduce inflammation.Make sure the ice pack does not rest on bare skin, so wrap a cloth/towel around it or place it over light clothing.

Compression will help to reduce inflammation. Wrap a compression bandage around the injured area and an ice pack too if practical, making sure you start the bandage well above and below the site of pain. Do not wrap the bandage so tight that you reduce blood flow!

Elevation – keep the injury elevated to reduce swelling.

Athlete's Foot

This is a fungal infection which shows itself as patches of red, itchy and scaly skin on the feet, particularly between the toes. It can cause the skin to crack which is painful and unattractive! If you think you may have athlete's foot treat it quickly because the warm, humid environment in your shoes encourages the fungus to grow making it more likely to spread from skin to nails and even other parts of the body.

Prevention and treatment

• Visit your pharmacy for a suitable treatment. There are many good creams and powders available.

• Keep your feet clean and dry.

- Reduce moisture further by using talcum powder.

- Change socks frequently.

- Either treat your shoes and socks, or consider buying new ones. Washing the socks may not be enough to kill the fungus.

Black toenail

This is caused by the impact of your toes pushing against the front of your shoe as you walk or sometimes general compression inside the shoe, particularly as your feet warm up as they can swell by a whole shoe size! This constant trauma can cause a blood blister to form under the nail, turning it black. If the blister is quite large it can push the toenail away from the nail bed. Quite often the nail will eventually fall off but a new one will grow back within a few months.

Prevention

As this is often caused by shoes that are too small, the first consideration must be shoes that fit well. Before you tie your laces slide your heel right in to the back of the shoe so that it is secure and does not slide as you walk. A thick pair of socks will help.

Treatment

See Dealing with blisters on page 92. If the problem is causing you discomfort, it would be advisable to consult your doctor or chiropodist/podiatrist.

Soft tissue injuries

Muscle strains

The main causes of muscle strains are fatigue and insufficient warm-up. In walkers, strains in the hamstring muscles located at the back of the thighs and the calf muscles are the most common. When soft muscle tissue is damaged, there may also be damage to local blood vessels causing bleeding into the nearby tissue. This causes swelling and pain in the area which can slow down healing. Reduce swelling by applying the RICE principles (see page 92) as soon as possible after the injury, to speed up the recovery and get you back walking. Most muscle strains in walkers are mild and should only require a few days rest but take care as a mild strain can become a moderate strain if you do not allow sufficient recovery time. Listen to your body – if you notice a niggle, do not try to push through it.

MUSCLE STRAIN	Symptoms	Treatment
First-degree tear/ mild strain	Local tenderness. You will probably be able to continue walking.	Rest as soon as possible and avoid walking until discomfort subsides, usually after a few days. Very gentle stretching
Second-degree tear/ moderate strain	Sudden sharp pain, often accompanied by swelling/ bruising and also loss of strength in the muscle. May be able to continue walking with difficulty.	Apply the RICE principles as soon as possible (see page 92). Anti-inflammatories may help. Visit your doctor or physiotherapist for diagnosis and further advice on strengthening and stretching.
Third-degree tear/ partial or total rupture (unusual in walkers)	Sudden sharp pain. May hear an audible 'snap' in the case of total ruptures. Depending on severity, muscle will lose all/most of its function. Bruising.	You need to seek medical attention immediately. A total rupture will require surgery.

I did a long walk yesterday and my muscles are sore today, am I injured?

This is probably delayed onset muscle soreness or 'DOMS' which is lots of tiny micro tears within your muscles. It will slow you down and weaken your muscles for a few days but it is not serious. If you feel that you may be getting sore after a long or challenging walk, cool the area down as soon as possible. Gentle activity and gentle stretching will also help. To avoid DOMS do not increase the length of your walks too quickly and make sure you warm-up and cool down properly.

Tendons and ligaments

A tendon is a continuation of a muscle and attaches muscle to bone. The Achilles tendon for example, is a continuation of your calf muscle and attaches to your heel bone. They are tough and fibrous but will stretch to a degree. A strain to the tendon is called tendonitis, or Achilles tendonitis in this case. The symptoms and methods of treatment are much the same as muscle strains, see table on page 94. However, the site of pain will often be over or around a bony area as this is the point at which the tendon attaches.

A ligament attaches bone to bone. They are not supposed to stretch as their job is to stabilize the joint to which they are attached. If they are overstretched this is called a 'sprain' and in walkers the most common site for a sprain is the ankle. If your foot suddenly turns over to one side, the ligaments on the other side will be stretched. If this is minor, it is still likely to be painful at the time but if you rest and apply the RICE method (see page 92) it should settle down in a few days. If you actually tear a ligament, it will be extremely painful, there will be swelling around the joint and weight-bearing will be difficult or impossible depending on the severity. Again apply the RICE method and seek medical advice. A really severe sprain resulting in a rupture of the ligament may need surgical intervention.

BONE INJURIES

Fractures

Compound fractures, i.e when you fall and break your arm, are uncommon in walkers. More likely, although still relatively uncommon, are stress fractures in the bones of the foot and tibia (shin bone). Stress fractures can occur in any bone which is constantly subjected to overload. This is one of the reasons why the training programmes in this book are progressive, allowing the body time to recover and strengthen, before the intensity increases. Replacing shoes every 560–800 kilometres will also help. If you feel pain or discomfort in the front of your foot which does not subside, you should seek medical advice. Sometimes a cast may be needed but more often than not it is a case of resting until it has healed. As with ligaments, bones do not have a good blood supply, so the healing process may take 4–8 weeks.

Shin splints

Shin splints can be a combination of bone and muscular trauma, but it is a general term used to describe painful shins. The muscles which run down the shin work hard to bring your toes up when you walk, particularly at higher speeds. If you are not used to walking, or you wear heels all day and then step into your flat trainers, these muscles will be unaccustomed to so much work and may complain! Other causes include weak shin or calf muscles, shoes with an inflexible sole or overstriding.

To prevent shin splints, build your distances gradually and warm up slowly for each walking session. Walking itself is a good way to strengthen the calf and shin muscles so the problem should improve as you progress. When you get back from your walks take time to do your stretches. If possible lie down and 'write' your name in the air with your toes to get the muscles at the front of your lower leg gently working and stretching. Use the RICE method (see page 92) to ease symptoms if you get back from a walk and your shins are sore.

> **Note**
> *If you experience a definite area of sharp pain in your shin this may be a sign of a stress fracture so visit your doctor for advice.*

Heat-related problems

Sunburn

Allowing your skin to burn in the sun is not only very uncomfortable in the short term but may also increase your risk of skin cancer in the long term, so you should take preventative measures.

• Don't walk outside between 11am and 3pm on hot summer days.

• Wear a peaked cap to protect your scalp and sunglasses which have full UV protection.

• Wear a waterproof sunscreen and make sure you put enough on and don't forget the tops of your ears, nose and shoulders. Reapply frequently.

• Don't leave large areas of skin exposed to the sun. Cover up with long sleeves and full-length trouser legs where possible and wear light colours and lightweight fabrics so you don't overheat. You can even buy clothes that have a built-in SPF.

If you get burnt

• Cool down burnt skin as quickly as possible. Get out of the sun, take a cool shower or apply a cold compress to the affected area.

- Use an aftersun cream or calamine lotion to soothe the skin.

- Drink lots of water.

- Consult a doctor if burns are severe.

Heat exhaustion

This condition is caused by the loss of water and salt loss through prolonged, excessive sweating. This is not a likely scenario when walking, but heat exhaustion can be very dangerous so you should be aware of the symptoms:

- Dizziness.

- Confusion.

- Nausea.

- Headache.

- Weak pulse but rapid, shallow breathing.

- Pale, clammy skin.

- Muscle cramps.

- Collapse.

What to do

You need to rest somewhere cool, get fluids and salts back in to your body and get medical help as soon as possible. If you are out walking you should have either a whistle in your bum bag to get attention or use your mobile telephone.

_____ **Replacing the salt** _____

If you are at home, dissolve 1 teaspoon of salt in 1 litre of water and keep sipping it.

Heatstroke

This can follow on from heat exhaustion and is caused by severe dehydration of the body. Sweating, which is a cooling mechanism, no longer occurs, meaning the body overheats to dangerous levels. It can develop very quickly and cause loss of consciousness and fitting, so urgent medical help is essential.

Symptoms include:
• Dizziness

• Confusion

• Headache

• Dilated pupils

• Fast pulse

• High fever and hot, dry skin

What to do
See Heat exhaustion, what to do, page 97, and call for medical help.

Cold-related problems

Hypothermia
Hypothermia occurs when the body temperature drops below 35°C (95°F). As a walker you are really only at risk from hypothermia if you are walking in extreme climates – mountainous regions for example where weather conditions could take you unawares. Serious injury which renders you immobile in very cold or wet conditions may also lead you to get very cold. Symptoms include:
• Shivering

• Pale, cold skin as blood is redirected away from the skin to vital organs

• Mood changes, e.g. confusion or overwhelming tiredness

• Slow pulse and slow shallow breathing

What to do
You need to get warm and dry as quickly as possible. Take a warm bath, get into bed and drink hot drinks to raise body temperature. If you are on your own you should let someone know that you are unwell. If necessary, seek medical help.

Other problems

Chafing

Chafing is irritated skin usually resulting from sweaty clothing rubbing against areas such as the inner thigh, armpits and nipples. Any of you who have already experienced this will know that it can be really sore for a few days. The advice is very similar to that given for blisters – prevention is better than cure!

Preventing chafing
- Make sure your clothes are a good fit, not too tight, not too loose. A snug fit is good, with as few seams as possible on the inside. If you are out walking and you feel a seam in your T-shirt rubbing, if decency allows, take it off and turn it inside out.

- Avoid wearing cotton and opt for clothes made from fibres that will wick moisture away from your skin such as Coolmax®.

- Avoid wearing new clothes for long walks.

- Try using a lubricant, such as petroleum jelly or one of the sports lubes available, on areas you know are prone to chafing.

Treatment
Once chafing has occurred, keep the affected area clean and covered to protect it from further irritation.

Bites and Stings

If you are allergic to certain insect stings make sure you have taken the necessary precautions before you set off for your walk. If you have an adrenaline injection pen, pack it in your bum bag and have your mobile phone with you so that you can get help if necessary.

If you do not suffer any allergic reactions, a bite or sting can still be quite unpleasant. In summer, think about wearing long-sleeved tops to keep skin covered and spray on some insect repellent before you leave home. Most stings can wait to be treated until you get home – apply an antihistamine lotion or cream. This also applies to nettle stings.

_____ **Natural antidote** _____

*Dock leaves often grow near stinging nettles and they really
do ease the burning sensation left by a sting. Pick a dock leaf*

and lay it over the effected area and the alkali in it will
neutralize the acid of the nettle sting.

Stitch

This is, quite literally, a pain. It usually presents itself in your side just at the bottom of your ribs and can take some time to subside. The exact cause of a stitch is the subject of much debate among scientists, but the most likely reason seems to centre around what is eaten and when, before exercise. The gut is connected to the diaphragm via ligaments. When we eat or drink the weight of the gut is increased which then stresses these ligaments.

How to avoid a stitch
• Avoid walking for 2–3 hours after a heavy meal or long drink.

• If you need to eat, keep it light and take small sips of fluid.

If you get a stitch
Bend forwards and pull your tummy button in to take the pressure off the ligaments involved.

Special considerations

In this section I'm going to cover pregnancy, asthma and back pain. There are other conditions that may give cause for extra consideration too.

NOTE: Whatever your personal circumstance, you should always seek the advice of a doctor before beginning any type of exercise programme. The following information is for general guidance only.

Walking during pregnancy

Keeping yourself fit when you are pregnant will not only help you with the pregnancy and the birth itself, but also afterwards when you have your little bundle to care for. Babies can be hard work! Fit mothers also tend to regain their pre-pregnancy shape and weight more quickly too. Walking is an excellent choice of exercise during pregnancy:

• It is a low-impact activity.

• Walking is cardiovascular, increasing the amount of oxygen coming into the body which will benefit mum and baby.

- Helps promote better sleep.

- Provides improved circulation, especially to the pelvic floor area.

- Helps improve body awareness and posture.

- You can continue walking all the way through the pregnancy if it is still comfortable to do so.

- Less chance of varicose veins developing.

- More positive outlook.

The key word when exercising during pregnancy is moderation. Make sure you warm-up and cool down properly (see pages 52–63). Don't walk too long, too far or too fast and especially not all three! Each stage of pregnancy, or trimester, brings with it different considerations.

First trimester (0–12 weeks)
During the first trimester you may feel quite tired and possibly sick, so take each day as it comes in terms of your walking.

- If you have any history of miscarriage you should mention this to your doctor when seeking their advice regarding walking for exercise.

- If you were already walking before you became pregnant, carry on as you were but just monitor intensity. You should be able to maintain short sentences when walking; if you are only able to gasp the odd word then you are working too hard.

- Make sure you don't walk for too long or when the weather is hot or humid and keep well hydrated to avoid overheating, which can be dangerous for the baby.

- During pregnancy the body releases a hormone called relaxin which softens ligaments in readiness for the birth. Ligaments are responsible for stabilizing the joints so avoid vigorous stretching.

- You should only do abdominal and core strength exercises at this stage if you are used to doing them. If not, follow the advice given for second trimester abdominal work. Remember moderation is the key. Not too many, not too hard.

Second trimester (13–28 weeks)
All the same considerations here as for the first trimester plus a few extra.

- Keep duration to 30 minutes or less and take rests where necessary.

- In your core strength work, avoid sit-up or 'crunch' type exercises as the main muscles involved are the *rectus abdominus*, which are already under stress as they try to accommodate the growing baby. Opt instead for strengthening the *transversus abdominus* muscles which are important postural muscles involved in supporting your back, and later, after having the baby, flattening your tummy again. Try this exercise. Get yourself into an all-fours position, with your hands about shoulder-width apart and your knees about hip-width apart. Make sure your back is in a neutral position. Maintaining this position, pull your tummy button up towards your spine and hold it there for about 20 seconds. It's very important that you don't hold your breath during this exercise, but it does take some practice to pull the tummy button in and breathe at the same time. Do this three times, then take a break, then do another three.

- As the baby increases in size there is a shift in your centre of gravity which may result in you arching your lower back more than normal. To combat this and avoid back ache, tuck your hips under you a little as you are walking. If you usually do some of your stretches on your back be aware that it may make you feel faint or lightheaded from about 20 weeks onwards. It is thought that the weight of the baby may reduce blood flow to the brain, and even to the baby itself, so lying on your back is best avoided. Generally, go with your instincts, but be aware that if you do start to feel lightheaded, you should alter your position.

3rd Trimester (28–40/42 weeks)
Follow all advice for the first and second trimesters plus the additional advice below:
- Listen to your body in this final trimester and don't push yourself too hard. If you feel tired the day after exercising, take a day off. Try to walk with a friend and if you are alone make sure someone knows where you are and when you will be back. Take a mobile phone with you too.

Pregnancy no no's

No marathons or long walks! Even if you take a marathon walk really steady it will still place a huge stress on your body and may result in you and the baby dangerously overheating. If you want to do a marathon use it as a long-term goal after your baby has been born.

Asthma

Asthma is a common condition affecting around three million people in the UK. Treatment usually involves the use of two types of inhalers – one to relax the muscles of the airways in the short term and one to reduce swelling of the airways in the longer term.

How can walking help?
Many asthmatics are put off exercise because they fear it may trigger an attack. While you need to be mindful of this, it is also true that being fit will help the body to cope with an attack. Seek your doctor's advice regarding exercise. You can start a walking programme at a low intensity and build up gradually. Try the beginners programme but use the rate of perceived exertion rather than monitoring your heart rate. This way you will always feel 'within' yourself. Repeat each week before moving on to the next to build your confidence.

Points to consider when walking
- It has been shown that warming up gradually can reduce the severity of airway muscle spasms.

- Breathing in cold air can be a trigger so consider walking on a treadmill when it is really cold outside though.

- Take your reliever inhaler out with you.

- Consider your route and use common sense. For example, if you know that pollen is a trigger for you, avoid walking past a field of oilseed rape; if you are sensitive to vehicle exhaust fumes don't walk through a busy town at rush hour.

- Enjoy it! Walking is a great way to relieve stress which itself can be a trigger for an attack.

Did you know?

You can strengthen your breathing muscles using a small handheld device called a POWERbreathe®. Studies have shown (McConnell et al. 1998 and Weiner et al. 1992) that strengthening breathing muscles appears to improve lung function and reduces asthma symptoms to the point where the use of a medicated inhaler is required less often. The good news is that you can gain most of the benefit within just a few weeks of use. There are three types of POWERbreathe®, so make sure you buy one that is suitable for you, and follow the instructions accordingly.

POWERbreathe®

Back Pain

Generally, walking is an ideal form of exercise if you have back pain but there are some back conditions that may be aggravated by it so have a chat with your doctor first.

How can walking help?

• Walking briskly will raise your heart rate and increase blood circulation, boosting oxygen and nutrient supplies to all the working muscles.

• Back pain can sometimes be caused by stress and anxiety. Walking is an ideal way to ease both.

• If you are overweight this places extra stress on your spine. Walking can help you to lose weight.

• Increase postural awareness and strengthen postural muscles.

Points to consider

• Warm-up and cool down thoroughly. Don't neglect your stretches at the end of your walk, particularly the hamstrings at the back of your thighs. Tight hamstrings can sometimes be the cause of back pain in the first place so stretching this muscle group is important.

• Maintaining good posture is vital. Make sure you are happy with this aspect of your walking before increasing your speed or distance. A common postural fault is to lean forward slightly from the hips which puts a lot of pressure on your lower back, so make sure you walk tall. Shoes with a negative heel, such as Masai Barefoot Technology®, can help you to walk upright. See page 29.

- If you are walking on a treadmill, try to avoid holding on as this can encourage a forward-leaning posture.

- Keep yourself well hydrated. Poor hydration levels can cause your back to ache as there is less fluid in the discs between each vertebra and therefore less cushioning from impact.

- Don't overdo it! Listen to your body and be patient. Have a look at the Beginner programme on page 66 and the core strength exercises on page 19 for some ideas.

Personal safety

'For safety is not a gadget but a state of mind'.
Eleanor Everet

Sadly we are not guaranteed safety whether we take our walks on the busiest streets or in the quietest country villages, but being aware of our surroundings and taking sensible precautions will reduce risk.

1. Plan your route and tell someone else where you are going and how long you expect to be gone for. When you are planning your route consider how you can cut the walk short if you need to. Are there shops nearby that you could go into if you needed to?

2. Equip yourself well (see page 25). You can store a panic alarm or whistle in your bum bag, just make sure you can get to it quickly.

3. Consider taking a mobile phone with you even if you don't usually use one. You can use it to store emergency phone numbers. Make sure it is fully charged and if it's 'pay as you go', ensure that it still has credit.

4. Don't take unnecessary risks, such as walking through a park on your own, whether you are male or female.

5. If you plan a long or difficult route or perhaps one that you haven't done before, don't do it alone. Take a friend along and give yourselves plenty of time to complete it before dark.

6. Try to avoid walking at night. If you do, don't walk alone and avoid secluded areas or anywhere that makes you feel uneasy. ALWAYS trust your instincts.

7. Walk confidently and be aware of what is going on around you. For general safety you could consider a course in self-defence.

8. Personal music systems are great for motivation and can be useful if you are walking on a treadmill, but for two reasons they should not be worn if you are walking outside: firstly you will be less aware of traffic and people approaching you and secondly, you may become the target of a mugging as these items are valuable.

9. Other valuable items such as jewellery or larger amounts of money should be left at home. The only money you should have with you is some loose change in case you need to use a public phone or want to buy a snack, bottle of water, etc.

10. Try to use pavements wherever possible but if you do have to walk on the road always face oncoming traffic and wear bright, light clothing with reflective panels so that you can be seen easily. This is the perfect excuse to wear your loudest, brightest training gear!

11. If you are unfortunate enough to be the victim of a mugging, don't try to fight back. You don't know how your attacker may react and when all is said and done they are after material possessions which can be replaced.

CHAPTER 7
GETTING THE FEELGOOD FACTOR

'Climb the mountains and get their good tidings.
Nature's peace will flow into you as sunshine
flows into trees. The winds will blow their
freshness into you, and the storms their energy,
while cares will drop off like falling leaves.'
John Muir

Whilst we can't all nip out for a walk in the mountains, with a little thought and planning we can get the most out of the area we live in. Walking close to nature has been shown to reduce stress and improve our sense of wellbeing so even if you live in the middle of a large city try to take part of your walk through a park or perhaps alongside a river. This chapter will give you some ideas on:

• Route planning/where to walk

• Ways to fit walking into your life

• Events

• Motivation

• Keeping a walking diary

PLANNING YOUR ROUTE

It is helpful to have a few regular routes that you know well so that you can use them to measure your progress, but equally don't forget that 'variety is the spice of life'. Not only will walking in different locations keep things interesting, it also gives you an opportunity to walk on different terrain which is good for your muscles. If you constantly change the way that you challenge your body it will reward you by becoming stronger and faster. Invest in an Ordnance Survey® map specially designed for walkers as these highlight trails and places of interest en route as well as other important information. This way you can identify areas of countryside, woodlands, lakes and rivers at a glance as a starting point.

Walking in town

Walking in towns gives you endless possibilities in terms of route variation so it has lots to offer. You are most likely to be walking on tarmac which is an unforgiving surface, so make sure your shoes have good cushioning. Try to pick pavements that are well maintained. Generally walking on predictable surfaces like pavements means you are less likely to sprain your ankles or knees but only if there aren't holes and rickety paving slabs! If you are walking in town at night make sure you go with someone else. You could also consider walking in shopping malls if you live near one. They can be enormous and have the added attraction of good lighting and an excellent walking surface. There are usually also plenty of toilets and telephone booths as well as places to buy food and drink if you get hungry afterwards!

Walking by rivers and lakes

There is something very therapeutic about walking around a lake or along a river tow-path. The sound and sight of even a relatively small piece of water can be very relaxing, whether it is listening to a babbling brook or admiring the stillness of a lake. Most of us live near some form of water so have a look at a map and investigate the possibilities.

Points to consider

• This may seem obvious but if you are walking around a lake make sure you know how far round it is! Sometimes trees and hedges obscure parts of lakes so the 'other side' can be much further than it first appears. Once you know this, ensure that you leave enough time to finish your walk in daylight.

• Some paths alongside rivers and lakes are busier than others. If you are in a very quiet area you would be well advised to walk with a friend.

• Paths are less likely to be tarmac so take care on uneven surfaces and make sure your shoes are still offering good support.

• Unless there is a designated swimming area you should avoid going into the water as it is often difficult to assess the depth and there may also be fast undercurrents.

Walking on the beach...

This is a real treat for all the senses – from the feel of sand between your toes to the sound of the waves crashing to shore. Sand is a great surface to walk on barefoot as each step needs to be stabilized by the muscles of the foot and lower leg in particular. However, if you aren't used to walking barefoot in sand (and most of us aren't) keep the duration short as it can cause the structures in your feet to overwork making them ache. The way around this is to either put your walking shoes back on or walk on hard, wet sand rather than soft, dry sand. Try walking in the water too as this provides useful resistance, maybe not in winter though!

...and along coastal paths

Often in areas of outstanding natural beauty, coastal paths offer some of the most spectacular and dramatic scenery in the country with lots of interesting sights along the way. They can also be quite challenging with steep ascents and descents so check a map before you set out. Check the weather forecast too as some areas of coastline can be very exposed. Make sure you take plenty of water and a snack as amenities can be few and far between, especially off season.

The countryside

The countryside offers the opportunity to walk in quieter surroundings which brings with it a real sense of calm. You can choose from trails and parks to local woodland and farm tracks. (Make sure you do not trespass.) Again it's well worth investing in an Ordnance Survey® map to help you plan a suitable route. It is more than likely that you won't meet anyone else during your walk and whilst it's nice to have the countryside to yourself you need to consider your safety if you are in an isolated spot. Try to walk with a companion and take precautions.

Other points to consider when planning your route
- Where possible try to make your walk a loop rather than simply turning round and coming back.

- Don't avoid the hills! Walking up hills is a good way to add some resistance work to your walks and increase your heart rate so don't avoid them! Think of the satisfaction and the view at the top.

Walking in groups

Joining a walking group can be a really good way to add interest and make new friends. This also has the obvious advantage of providing security, particularly if this is something that concerns you. The social aspect is important as your fellow walkers can offer you support and encouragement, as well as friendship. If you have access to the Internet this is a good place to start looking for a local group. Walking holidays can be a really good way to see more of a country and there are many to choose from – it could be hiking in the Lake District or walking to Everest Base Camp! If you plan to go on a walking holiday make sure you ask lots of questions first to ensure that it is suitable for you and that you are fully prepared for the daily itinerary.

FITTING WALKING INTO YOUR LIFE

The programmes in Chapter 5 are based around a structured routine that you will need to allow time for. You may feel you are not ready for a programme just yet but would still like to increase your activity levels in readiness. Remember, we should aim to take at least 10,000 steps each day, particularly if weight loss is the goal. Below are some suggestions as to how you can include more walking in your everyday life. Don't forget to wear your pedometer so you can log your progress.

At work

If you work in an office, you may have to use your imagination a little but try these ideas for starters.

- If you use a bus or train, get off at an earlier stop and walk the rest of the way

- Park your car as far away from your office as you can and walk back.

- Don't send so many e-mails to people in the same office. Although convenient, they do stop you from making those short trips to see your colleagues and the lost steps soon add up.

- If lunch is usually delivered to you, go out for a walk and get it yourself instead. You'll also feel better for the fresh air.

At home

- Cleaning and tidying! Not everyone's favourite pastime, but a good way to increase your activity levels, particularly if it involves going up and down the stairs a few times.

- If you have toilets upstairs and downstairs, use the one upstairs.

- Do some gardening.

- Hide the remote control.

- If you have a dog and usually walk once a day, go for another one. Many dogs need more exercise than they get and are only too pleased to go for a second walk. Don't forget the poop-scoop though!

Out and about

- Use stairs instead of lifts or escalators. If you have to use an escalator, walk up it.

- If you have a short and a long route, always pick the longer one if time allows.

- Walk to visit a friend.

- Go shopping!

- If you have children, walk to the park and play with them.

MOTIVATION

We all know the importance of taking regular exercise to keep fit and healthy and that we'll feel better once we've made the effort, but all too often, particularly when the weather is bad or life gets a bit too hectic, we give in just a little too easily to our lazy side – everybody has one! The problem is the weather is often less than perfect and we lead hectic lives, so if we wait for everything to be perfect we'd never go walking! Here are some thoughts to help you out of the door:

- Firstly, just remind yourself of all the benefits of a walking programme (see page 47).

- Make an appointment with yourself, put it in your diary or calendar and stick to it as you would for any other appointment. If that doesn't work, make an appointment with a friend as you are less likely to move it or change plans.

- Set goals and reward yourself when you achieve them.

- If you are following a programme, try not to look beyond the week that you are on. In fact if you are new to exercise, just take it one day at a time. If you haven't exercised for years, it will take time to build your new habit into your life.

- Why are you walking? When it's wet, cold and windy outside you will need to dig deep and remember what it was that inspired you to walk in the first place. Is it to lose weight for a specific event? Is it because your health is letting you down? Are you entered for a walking event? Find a picture, photograph or quote that inspires you and reminds you why you are walking and put it somewhere prominent, such as on the front door or the fridge.

- Keep boredom at bay by varying the route you take.

- If your day has got the better of you try this. Put on your walking shoes and just tell yourself you'll do a quick 5 minutes. The chances are you'll feel better almost straightaway and complete your whole walk!

- If you have been unwell or you have had to take some time out from your walking programme, don't be disheartened. It won't take long to get back into your stride. Remember to be positive. You can't change what has already happened so don't dwell on it!

- When the weather is bad, embrace it! Get wrapped up and enjoy it rather than using it as an excuse not to go out. If you get muddy and wet it doesn't really matter and it can be quite refreshing.

- Visualization. This is a technique often used by athletes who learn to think positively about every aspect of their performance, from warming-up right through to a strong finish and collecting their medal! Positive visualisation keeps negative 'self talk' to a minimum. You should always imagine yourself as being the person you want to be rather than dwelling on the things that you don't want.

Positive thinkers are estimated to live longer than people who always see the negative side of things. So, don't walk along wishing you were thinner and cursing the thoughtless driver who just drove through a puddle and soaked you to the skin five minutes after you left home. Turn it around in your mind. You were out looking and feeling so great that a driver didn't see the huge puddle in the road and drove straight through it soaking you, but you're having a great day so it doesn't matter!

EVENTS

There are so many events on offer up and down the country, both competitive and non competitive so take advantage and use them to keep you motivated and focused. Distances on offer vary from short walks to full marathons to treks in far-flung destinations so pick an event that suits your ability and if you think it's a little beyond what you can do right now, make it a goal, get out there and train for it! Why not choose a charity close to your heart and raise some money for them at the same time so that as many people as possible benefit from your walking.

KEEPING A DIARY

I'd recommend that you keep a steps log and a diary. Get yourself a notepad and customize it to suit.

Record the following:

- The date and time of your walk.

- Your route.

- Distance/number of steps/time.

- Intensity – not just your heart rate if you are using a monitor, but also how you felt as you were walking. Was it easy, hard or just right?

- Speed – if you know your distance and how long it took you can work out your speed, although a pedometer will also give you this information.

- Weight loss – if you are making a conscious effort to lose weight it can be helpful to record it, although it would be better to make this a weekly entry rather than a daily one.

- Details about the weather. This will help with future comparisons. If you are comparing two identical walks and one was done on a fine, still day whilst the other was done in a roaring headwind then it won't come as a surprise to you if your windy walk was a little slower!

- Other information – leave yourself room to make general comments about how you felt physically and emotionally during your walk. Perhaps you find a particular route really uplifting or maybe those new socks just weren't comfortable. These things are always interesting to look back on and more importantly, you can learn from past experiences.

Steps Log

Add up your total steps for each week and plot the totals on simple chart like this so you can see your progress.

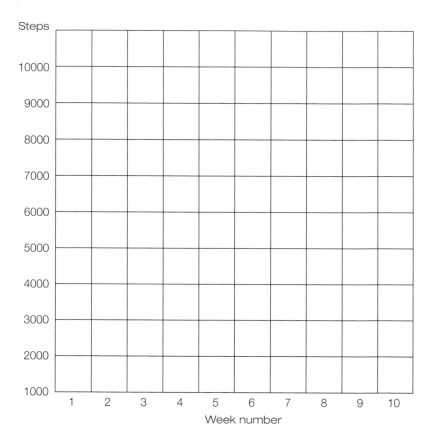

Walking diary

Date/ Time	Route	Distance/ No. of steps/ Time/	Intensity - % HRM RPE	Weight 66 kg goal	Weather	Comments
12/03/07 9 am	Church loop	3.5 km 35 mins 3800 steps	60% MHR RPE 11 – easy	68 kg	Windy but sunny about 12°C	Strong headwind going up Church Path. Nice day, felt good. Left calf tight.

CHAPTER 8
FUELLING YOUR WALKS

'The wise man should consider that health
is the greatest of human blessings.
Let food be your medicine.'
Hippocrates

What to eat or what not to eat can be very confusing especially as hardly a week goes by without some new 'wonder' diet being thrust under our noses. There are some tips in this section that will help if you're trying to lose weight but, if you eat a diet high in nutritional quality, you are likely to find that you lose some weight when you start walking anyway. This is not only down to the food itself but how it makes you feel – if you eat a healthy diet this will be reflected in your energy levels. You will be more likely to join in with the childrens' football game or do an extra loop around the shopping centre, for example.

Top tips for healthy eating

Positive thinking

Often when people are talking about their eating habits they will tell you about all the things they shouldn't have because they're 'bad'. No one food is that bad for you, it's more about the way we combine them over a period of time that is the problem. Concentrate on the things you should be eating more of, rather than thinking about all the things you 'can't' have. If you make particular foods out of bounds you will end up wanting them even more!

Eat more complex carbohydrates

Complex carbohydrates are grain-based foods, such as wholegrain and wholemeal breads, brown rice, porridge oats and muesli. Because these foods haven't been heavily processed, they are packed with energy-giving B vitamins and fibre, as well as providing you with a low-fat source of energy. Complex carbohydrates also tend to be high in fibre which satisfies our appetite and a good source of dietary fibre. Simple carbohydrates found in white breads, white rice and white pasta will have been stripped of much of their nutritional value so keep these to a minimum in your diet.

Consider your fat intake

But don't be obsessed about it. We need a certain amount of fat in our diet. Some key facts about fat:

- Is stored in adipose tissue under the skin and is a vital source of energy.

- Fat plays an important part in cell structure.

- Helps hormone production.

- Protects and cushions our vital organs.

Saturated fats – found in large amounts in meat and dairy products, cakes, biscuits and pastry. Reduce the amount of this type of fat in your diet as it can raise blood cholesterol levels, a risk factor associated with high blood pressure and heart disease. Think about the total nutritional package too. If you had to make a choice between a small piece of cheese and a shop bought biscuit, go for the cheese because it contains other useful nutrients too.

Trans fats – even worse than saturated fats for increasing cholesterol levels. These are a by product of a process called hydrogenation, which is when oils are turned into solid fats. Trans fats are commonly found in pastry, cakes, confectionery and biscuits. If you see the words 'hydrogenated vegetable oil' in the ingredients list, the chances are that it will contain trans fats, so avoid it whenever possible.

Unsaturated fats – these are better for us and can actually lower cholesterol. Foods high in unsaturated fats include nuts and seeds; oily fish such as salmon, fresh tuna, trout and mackerel; vegetable oils; olive oil and avocados. Oily fish in particular are a good source of Omega 3 and 6 fatty acids which have been shown to offer protection against heart disease. These magic fats, in particular Omega 3 fatty acids, are also important for:

- Maintaining good brain and eye function.

- Keeping joints healthy.

- Improved endurance and energy levels.

If you are vegetarian you can increase your intake of Omega 3 and 6 fatty acids by using linseed oil in cooking or by grinding up seeds like pumpkin and sunflower and adding them to cereals, soups and smoothies.

Go natural

Reward your body with natural, unrefined foods wherever possible and try to avoid processed foods such as ready-meals and convenience foods that are likely to contain frightening amounts of salt and fat and little else. Don't expect your body to perform well for you if you don't give it the necessary building blocks. Use organic fruit, vegetables and milk wherever possible and buy free range organic eggs, meat and poultry. They will invariably be of higher nutritional quality and in the case of meat and poultry, welfare standards will also be better. This may seem expensive but if you start to cook your own meals, you can use the best ingredients and often the result is less expensive than buying a ready-prepared meal.

Five-a-day and go bright!

Make sure you have at least five portions of fruit and vegetables each day to maximize your intake of vitamins, minerals and fibre. Go for lots of different brightly-coloured fruits and vegetables such as broccoli, tomatoes and blueberries that are brimming with natural chemicals called phytonutrients, thought to offer protection against cell damage and some cancers. A portion is:

• One apple, banana, orange or pear

• One large handful of any berries

• A salad

• Three tablespoons of cooked carrots or peas

• One glass of orange juice (although five glasses doesn't mean five portions – orange juice does not contain all the fibre of a whole orange).

Include fruits and vegetables in soups, stews and smoothies; raw with a dip; as a side dish and in salads and fruit salads.

Never skip breakfast

You won't have eaten since the previous evening so a hearty breakfast is an important start to your day. If you get it right your breakfast will see you through to mid-morning; get it wrong and you'll be tired and irritable. Eating a cereal rich in complex carbohydrates, such as porridge or muesli, will ensure a steady release of energy throughout the morning as they are low/medium GI foods (see box below). If you find it difficult to eat in the mornings try making a smoothie instead by blending up some fruit with a little yogurt. You could also invest in a juicer. Bear in mind that the fibre of the fruit is often left behind so don't have all your fruit as juice.

What does GI mean?

GI stands for glycaemic index. Foods containing carbohydrates are rated from 0–100 according to how quickly it is broken down and released as glucose into the blood stream. Below are the GI values for some common foods:

FOOD	Glycaemic Index	
Grapefruit	25	Low
Whole milk	27	
Dried apricots	31	
Porridge with water	42	
Baked beans	48	
Muesli	56	
Basmati rice	58	Medium
Raisins	64	
Shredded wheat	67	
White bread	70	
Cheerios®	74	High
French fries	75	
Cornflakes	84	
White rice	98	

Which foods are best?

Foods which have a low to medium GI keep us feeling satisfied for longer, whereas foods with a high GI can cause a sudden rush of sugar into the bloodstream. The body releases insulin to control it and often the result is blood sugar levels lower than when you ate the food, which just makes you feel tired and hungry all over again!

So are foods with a high GI bad?

Not necessarily. There are times, if you have been out for a long brisk walk for example, when your body needs energy quickly to replenish its stores. In this case it's a good idea to eat a relatively high GI snack. Food eaten within 20–30 mins of vigorous exercise is also less likely to be stored as fat.

What should I eat before a walk?
Eating a medium to low GI snack about two hours before
your walk will give you enough time to digest it and top up
your energy levels. A couple of slices of wholemeal toast with
a scraping of honey would be perfect.

Top tips for weight loss

This should really be called fat loss and not weight loss. If you are taking regular exercise you may put on a little weight as you will increase the amount of muscle in your body (muscle weighs more than fat). You can put on weight but still lose body fat. This is what makes your waistband feel looser regardless of what the scales may say! Fat loss is best achieved through a combination of exercise and healthy eating. Walking will raise your metabolism so that you burn more calories and sensible, healthy eating will encourage your body to give up its fat supplies and work with you.

You should also read the Top tips for healthy eating on page 116, as they will all help.

Keep a food diary

Record everything you eat and drink, and at what time, over a 5–7 day period and try to include a weekend day. Look back at your diary at the end of the week and see if any patterns emerge. Do you always come home from work starving and eat several chocolate biscuits with a cup of tea and two sugars? Sometimes these things become such ingrained habits we don't even realize we do it. Add up how many biscuits, packets of crisps or chocolate bars you have over a week and you'll be amazed at how many calories they can provide. It's not just that these kinds of foods are calorific but also they don't provide any nutritional benefit either. Even worse, sugary refined foods can rob our body of essential nutrients used in order to process them.

Eat smaller, more regular meals

This will encourage your body to give up its fat supplies more easily. If you leave long gaps between meals, your body goes into a 'famine mode'. The metabolism slows down and fat is stored rather than used for immediate energy. These are both the opposite of what we want to achieve – we want a faster metabolism and a body that burns fat readily.

Aim to lose weight slowly

Try not to lose too much weight in a week. If you are losing lots of weight quickly you may be losing lean tissue i.e muscle. Since lean tissue is five times more metabolically active than fat tissue you need to keep as much of it as possible! The good news is that your walking is likely to be building lean tissue.

Be prepared
Take your own lunch to work with you so you can pack healthy choices. Include some healthy snacks too so that if you get hungry you don't have to rush to the nearest vending machine!

Know your body
Learn to recognize when you are truly hungry and have a healthy snack rather than waiting until you are starving and grab anything. Quite often we confuse hunger with thirst, so if you feel hungry have a glass of water and see how you feel. If you still feel hungry, get yourself something to eat.

Watch your alcohol intake
Carbohydrates and protein provide about 4Kcals per gram, fat provides 9Kcals and alcohol provides 7Kcals so just a couple of glasses of wine can be 250–300Kcals. To put this into perspective, that's about what you would burn if you walked briskly for an hour. Moderation is the key here.

Make a smoothie!
Fresh smoothies are packed full of vitamins and nutrients in a form that is really easy for our bodies to digest. They are also very filling, particularly if you include some banana or natural yogurt.

Stay hydrated

Why we need water
Water is vital for our survival making up 60–70% of our total body weight. Water:

• Supplies our cells with nutrients and takes waste away from them.

• Maintains body temperature and fluid balance.

• Maintains a healthy digestive system.

• Keeps skin clear and radiant.

• Helps to maintain energy levels and mental clarity.

How we lose water	approx. ml per day
Skin and breathing	900
Sweat	50 (when not exercising)
Faeces	100
Urine	1500

this adds up to 2550 millilitres before we have done any exercise! When we exercise, our breathing and sweating rates increase and consequently further fluid is lost. During intense exercise athletes can lose between four and five litres of fluid an hour.

If we don't replace lost fluid

If we lose more fluids than we are taking in, dehydration will occur. In it's early stages it can cause dizziness, headaches, tiredness, irritability, anxiety and nausea. In the warm summer months you need to be aware of these symptoms because if dehydration is left untreated, it can progress to more serious conditions such as heat exhaustion.

Preventing dehydration

To avoid the effects of dehydration you will need to think about fluid intake before, during and after your walking session. Unfortunately it's not enough to rely on your sense of thirst, as usually by this time we can already be at 1–2% dehydration which can result in a 5–10% reduction in performance.

- On any given day try to drink at least two litres of water. If you are exercising you will need to drink more. Try filling a two-litre bottle of water and make sure you finish it by the end of the day. Little and often is the key here rather than drinking large amounts all at once.

- Have a glass of warm (boiled, then allowed to cool) water in the morning with half a slice of lemon – this is a good cleanser for the kidneys and unlike coffee or tea contains no caffeine.

- Keep your fruit and vegetable intake high as they have a high water content and have the added advantage of containing lots of vitamins and minerals.

Before your walk

For short walks of 20 minutes or less, just making sure you are well hydrated before you leave will suffice. See box opposite. It is still a good idea to take a bottle of water with you though, particularly if it is hot or, in case you are tempted to stay out longer. For longer walks, make sure you are well hydrated and have a drink just before you leave. How much you drink is really a matter of personal preference –

some people find they are more susceptible to getting a stitch if they drink too much too close to their walking session.

_____ **A wee check for dehydration** _____

A reliable way to tell if you are well hydrated or not is to
assess the colour of your urine. If it is very light, almost clear,
your hydration levels are good. If it is dark yellow you need
take some water on board.

During your walk

Take a bottle of water with you and make a point of taking small regular drinks from it. You should do this even in winter, as you will still lose fluids during exercise. If it's hot or humid, or you are out for a long walk of over an hour, you may even want to use an isotonic sports drink as these contain electrolytes to replace lost body salts. See below.

After your walk

If you have been taking regular drinks whilst on your walk, a glass of water on your return will be enough. How much water you need to drink really depends how much you lose and this will vary from one person to the next, and from one day to the next. You can occasionally weigh yourself before and after your walk, making sure you are wearing the same clothes, and the difference will be what you have lost in water. You will need to drink 1.5 times the amount lost to fully replace your fluids so if you lost 400 millilitres you would need to drink about 600 millilitres as replacement.

Does it have to be water?

You don't have to drink water exclusively, but some drinks are better at hydrating our bodies than others.

Drink	Suitability
Tap water	Ideal. This is closely monitored for impurities. If your tap water is heavily chlorinated (you can sometimes smell it) try using a water filter which will remove it.
Bottled water	These are fine from a hydrating point of view, but recent research suggests that chemicals from the bottles may leach into the water, which is not desirable. Check the source too as some bottled waters are just tap water repackaged.

Sports drinks	If you are trying to lose weight be aware that most of these drinks will contain carbohydrate for energy. For most walks under an hour, unless you are doing particularly intense interval training, a sports drink is unnecessary, but some people find them easier to drink than water alone. If you suspect you are dehydrated, these drinks are ideal as they replace lost fluids quickly.
Tea/coffee	These can count towards your fluid intake but be aware that they contain caffeine which is a diuretic in large amounts and can cause the body to lose water. One or two cups a day is fine.
Fizzy drinks	Not a good idea whilst walking as the bubbles can cause heart burn and general gastric discomfort. Apart from water, many of these drinks are also very high in sugar.
Fruit juice	Fruit juice is fine; but dilute it 50/50 with water as it is too concentrated on its own. If you add a half to one teaspoon of salt you have made your own sports drink!
Flavoured waters	Often laden with sweeteners and sugar, these drinks are not a good substitute for plain water. It's better to flavour plain water with a drop of squash or cordial.

USEFUL RESOURCES

British Heart Foundation
14 Fitzhardinge St
London
W1H 6DH
020 7935 0185
www.bhf.org.uk
Advice on walking for a healthy heart.

Fletcher Sport Science
15 Coldicot Gardens
Evesham
Worcestershire
WR11 2JW
www.fletchersportscience.co.uk
Fitness testing, Suunto heart rate
monitors and POWERbreathe®

National Trust
PO Box 39
Warrington
WA5 7WD
www.nationaltrust.co.uk
Suggested walks.

Ordnance Survey
Customer Service Centre
Romsey Road
Southampton
SO16 4GU
www.ordnancesurvey.co.uk
For all things map-related.

The Ramblers Association
2nd floor, Camelford House
87-90 Albert Embankment
London
SE1 7TW
www.ramblers.org.uk
Tips, events and group walks.

www.exerciseregister.org
Will help you find a qualified fitness
professional.

www.go4awalk.com
Lots of walking ideas, from routes to
equipment.

www.lessbounce.com
Specializing in sports bras.

www.walkingbritain.co.uk
Over 6,000 pages of walking
information.

www.walking-routes.co.uk
Good for finding walks in your area,
with lots of information on local points
of interest and wildlife.

www.whi.org.uk
Initiative to get people walking.

Acknowledgements

I would like to thank Clare Hubbard for giving me the opportunity to write this book. Thanks must also go to Eddie Fletcher at Fletcher Sport Science who is a constant source of inspiration to me. Thank you to my friends and family who have been supportive and encouraging throughout, and finally a huge thankyou to my husband Kevan, whose patience knows no bounds!

Index